Village Hours

VILLAGE
HOURS

RONALD BLYTHE

CANTERBURY
PRESS
N·o·r·w·i·c·h

© Ronald Blythe 2012

First published in 2012 by the
Canterbury Press Norwich
Editorial office
3rd Floor, Invicta House,
108-114 Golden Lane,
London EC1Y 0TG

Canterbury Press is an imprint of Hymns Ancient and Modern Ltd
(a registered charity)
13A Hellesdon Park Road, Norwich,
Norfolk, NR6 5DR, UK

www.canterburypress.co.uk

British Library Cataloguing in Publication data

A catalogue record for this book is available
from the British Library

ISBN 978 1 84825 237 0

Printed and bound in Great Britain by
CPI Group (UK) Ltd, Croydon

Contents

For David Holt

JANUARY

The Approaching Snow

APPROACHING SNOW. I think I can smell it. The fields ache in the cold. A brave band of chrome yellow straight out of my old paintbox streaks across the sky. All the trees are still. At matins, 16 of us crowd into the chancel to keep warm, like Bishop Heber's beasts of the stall. I expect that poor young man, torrid in India, longed for snow.

What we have to learn is to work at home during snow. Commuters should have a winter desk in their houses where, with today's gadgetry, they could turn in a good day's toil without struggling through drifts to the office. Schoolchildren, too. Approaching snow might be when the value of a meeting could be assessed.

Why is Duncan flying the Australian flag on his barn? It is a flag in shock. It flaps stiffly towards the freezing North Sea. I write with my back to what is to come because it will be, as always, strangely thrilling. David telephones. Have I got bread? He can get down in the Land Rover. The cat, languorous between curtain and glass, trades whiteness with whiteness.

Preaching at New Year, in quiet mid-flow on Doctor Johnson's resolutions, I have a feeling that I have done so before. It cannot be helped, however. And, anyway, that great

Christian man should be heard alongside the Epiphany manifestation. He was an old man who could not change his ways. And, indeed, why should he?

He had practised his faith at huge inconvenience to himself. 'I have taken my wife's unpleasant friend into my house. I have taken a black boy into my house, fed him, taught him, and made him my son.'

Samuel Johnson was following the epistle of Paul to Philemon to the letter. And yet, like some January fool, he would resolve:

To apply to study.
To rise early.
To go to church.
To drink less.
To oppose laziness.
To put my books in order.

My mother told me how she would look up at his statue – a clumsy figure staring towards Fleet Street – when she went to Sunday school at St Clement Danes. He loved Christ, wrote beseeching prayers, and dismissed the Church's everlasting arguments with: 'Sir, I think all Christians, whether Papists or Protestants, agree in the essential articles, and that their differences are trivial, and rather political than religious.'

The snow is now very near. Fragments of the Christmas fall wait in the ditches to welcome it. The clouds cannot move. The roses rattle. With the oil tank full and the log-corner high with split ash, and the fridge still mildly bursting, I feel like the husbandman and his eat, drink, and be merry. Wonderful leftovers. What is more delectable than a half-eaten pie?

After the cards come the invites to the year's literature festivals, the requests to do this and that, the need to read, the services for Lent, and, in the year's good time, the spring flowers.

Distant friends ring. 'Are you snowed in? We are thinking of you.' How impatient they are.

'When that I was and a little tiny boy'

A MEDIEVAL KING would 'keep his Christmas' at Woodstock or Westminster, or wherever he happened to be. And God keeps us, wherever we happen to be. 'Keep me as the apple of the eye.' James I liked to keep his Christmas at Whitehall, a vast palace of which only Inigo Jones's banqueting hall remains. Fresh from Scotland, no longer scalded by its Kirk, James was alternately entertained, if that is the description, by Lancelot Andrewes and William Shakespeare. The mighty Bishop at the beginning of the feast, the peerless writer at its end. The sermon kept to the solemn rules with a vengeance; the often disgraceful court pulled itself together; the play, *Twelfth Night*, kept it entranced. Rarely were there such festivities as these. They were talked about for months afterwards. In his Christmas sermon, Andrewes's learnedness would sometimes forsake him, rather as the intellectuality of the Wise Men would forsake them as they entered the stable. Like every good preacher, he knew when to abandon the script. Or, rather, he knew that there would be moments in the gospel story when he would go to pieces. Thus there began those emotional unscripted asides in the retelling of it.

3

Nobody was more understanding than James, for whom the word 'baby' was so wonderful that he went on calling his son and lover this when they were in their 20s, signing his letters to them, 'Your Dad and Gossip'. Seated below the pulpit, he heard Bishop Andrewes approaching the stable on Christmas morning with his theology pat, his severe face all set for the great occasion, his notes crackling in his hand. And then – a new-born boy. The Saviour of mankind. The preaching went out of his voice, King and court went silent. Not a sound in the freezing chapel. But Andrewes was not in it; he was in Bethlehem. 'An infant – the infant Word – the Word without a word – the eternal Word not able to speak a word – a wonder sure . . .'

Then, almost a fortnight later, it would all end with *Twelfth Night*, the holiness, the feeding, the exhaustion – and the order. For the latter was strictly enforced, whatever else occurred. *Twelfth Night* was misrule, when the sacred pattern was reversed, and rich and poor, and male and female exchanged roles. It was wild. But so would the climate be, until springtime, dark and cold and deathly.

For a few hours, dukes would become servants, boys would become girls. Being divine, kings could not become anything else, of course. James watched his Players perform *Twelfth Night*, a final Christmas entertainment which Mr Shakespeare had written especially for him, and, maybe, Bishop Andrewes watched it too.

Christmas had been a box of gifts, *Twelfth Night* was a box of tricks. In between were the parties and the worship. Now had come the reckoning. It is not quite Christmas Eve, however, and neither the Boy born to be King nor the bills are with us. In the Suffolk market-town, an immense conifer sways and glitters.

4

Teenagers who have not as yet been shown any of the wear and tear of Christmas look beautiful under the swaying lights. The clergy are looking to their laurels as they hurry from Nine Lessons to Nine Lessons, and from Midnight to Midnight. The bells, some of them as old as Shakespeare, rock in the towers. One should long since have been surfeited with all this. How does it stay so fresh? How do babies cause one to be at a loss for words? How strange it all is.

Ivy

FORGET the economy: the big question is: can I say at St Andrew's this Sunday what I said at SS Peter and Paul last Sunday? Would this be sloth, or a fair distribution of genius? The white cat sits in the window, grumbling at green woodpeckers devouring Waitrose chicken scraps. It really is the limit.

The day is grey and sweet. The wood is full of snowdrops. The study is piled with books. Epiphany is fading into Before Lent. There isn't a sound except little animal-grousings.

Ivy has brought down a pond-side ash, and Richard is coming to clear it. It reminds me of Thomas Hardy's poem 'His Ivy Wife', in which a woman clings so suffocatingly to her husband that she brings him down.

Among the world's serious divisions are those who are at ease with ivy on trees and those who are not. I have an ancient ash on which ivy has created or founded a kind of leaf city for countless creatures. It feeds on pond water, and generously sheds dead boughs for kindling. It has been here for ever – since

1900, say. It sings along with its birds. 'That'll fall on you one of these days.' Well. It used to be pronounced 'ivery' in this part of England. 'That ivery, that want to come down.'

Its grown-up name is Hedera helix. It is magical and sad at the same time, glossy and dark, mournful and – to me – happy enough. To quote what Geoffrey Grigson quoted from an 18th-century gardening manual, ivy goes with ruins as excellently as bacon goes with eggs, and the 20th-century policy of stripping it off them has entirely altered our sightseeing.

You will not encounter the following any more. Thomas Whatley (any relation to the archbishop?) is at Tintern Abbey in 1770:

> The shapes of the windows are little altered; but some of them are quite obscured, others partially shaded, by tufts of ivy, and those which are most clear are edged with slender tendrils, and lighter foliage, wreathing about the sides and divisions; it winds round the pillars; it clings to the walls; and in one of the aisles, clusters at the top in bunches so thick and so large, as to darken the space below . . .
>
> Nothing is perfect; but memorials in every part still subsist; all certain but all in decay; and suggesting, at once, every idea which can occur in a seat of devotion, solitude and desolation . . . No circumstance so forcibly marks the desolation of a spot once inhabited, as the prevalence of nature over it. In ruins, an intermixture of a vigorous vegetation intimates a settled despair of their restoration.

Put away your Pevsner; find your prayer. Soon William Wordsworth would be standing below this architectural growth.

The Duke of Hamilton used to live in Suffolk, this not so long ago. His old gamekeeper once told me that 'Park Cottage' – the gamekeeper's home – 'was situated close to Maids Wood. It was strongly built of brick covered with ivy. It was always the Duke's wish to have ivy planted against any houses which he had built. Also, when planting new plantations, to have ivy put against each tree. His Grace loved ivy.'

The Duke also had a crinkle-crankle brick wall that serpentined for miles, and is a wonder still. Attitudes towards ivy have been ambivalent since classical times, says my friend Richard Mabey.

Just a few lines . . .

DRIVING to church through the melted snow lakes, we very nearly brake with astonishment. Duncan has laid his mainly hawthorn hedge. Not given it what-ho! with what his father used to call 'the murderer' – the machine that did as much in an hour as the old winter workers with their 'hooks' did in a week. Tree-size growth has been sawn off, and pliable side-branches have been semi-cut and woven into a living basketwork.

Now I know why Duncan surveyed my sky-touching hazel so accusingly. 'John [Nash] could paint my ploughing from your garden. Now it would be invisible.'

This sublimely overgrown hedge-hazel is what I look through at about six each morning to get my bearings, as one might put it. I drink tea, and dream through its January fretwork, which is already fuzzy with catkins. But Duncan isn't going to swallow this airy-fairy explanation for permitting hedge hazel to grow as high as an oak. Nor at this moment had I known about his hedge-laying. But how good it is. A lesson to us all.

On Friday, I give a lecture to the Cambridge University Extension class in Sudbury. Mature students. The momentary singing in my ears comes from the great saw in the timber-yard which filled the little town with its howls when I was a boy. Our classroom stands on the spot.

Our subject is the literature of the Second World War, plus its personal correspondence. This was the last of the Parker-pen and HB-pencil letter, the indelible-ink diary, the need to put pen to paper every day. I am in the midst of describing this wonderful activity when it dawns on me that I am addressing a generation who would have done this. But old men – and ladies – forget. Those were the days when the advert for the job said: 'Apply in writing'; and when, as I discovered in the vast cache of forces' letters and journals in the Imperial War Museum library, people with no education to speak of wrote master-pieces. For it was unthinkable not to be able to write a letter. And impossible to reach a mother or lover by any other means.

Outside, it gently rained. Back home, the birds complained wetly on the snow-sodden grass, and were thrown old mince pies.

Visitors arrived to talk about a house in Cornwall. It is rare to get a Cornish house out of one's head. This one had begun as a cell for medieval monks, descended into a poor little farm, moved sideways into the ownership of a poet, and now glowed a bit under the protection of an artist.

It used to be my base for starting out to Bodmin Moor, or to where Thomas Hardy courted his Emma. Not one grey stone of it could be rubbed out. A waterfall crashed into a ravine near by. Delabole slates furnished the ground floor as well as the roof.

And the garden was walled-in with 'hedges', those timeless Cornish barriers that are often so thick with wild flowers that their granite structure is entirely hidden.

Valerian, campion, primroses, nests, and, in May, white waving barriers of sheep's parsley. And, underneath, the new stone. Any ancient Cornish settlement has enough shaped granite on it to build another house. Here, at Treneague, the Atlantic roared within walking distance – well, a pretty long walk.

A Reunion

ANTONY arrived all the way from Pickering, and the following day, knowing his passion for sites, which is so like my own, I asked: 'Where would you like to go? What would you like to see?' And quick as a flash he said: 'Dorothy L. Sayers's house in Witham.' The strangest feeling then not so much overcame me as stopped me in my local-guide tracks.

I saw a young man, nervously awaiting the arrival of a famous author, and her mounting the staircase to the crowded lecture-room, monocle glittering, no notes in hand – a middle-aged woman whose kindness was matched with great learning and some amusement. It was myself and Sayers, long, long ago.

She was to give a talk on the Emperor Constantine and his Colchester-born mother, Helena. Evelyn Waugh would write a novel about Helena. It seems she was all the rage. Sayers and I later attended a vast, pageant-like play she had written about Constantine, and I can still see her somewhat forbidding charm.

Antony and I found her house in Witham and, opposite it,

her bronze statue. It was the only time I have stood beside the statue of someone I had sat beside. There was a nice bronze cat, which may have been the one on Lord Peter Wimsey's coat of arms.

And in the wonderful public library, created from an old cinema, was a fine centre for a writer who had not only invented one of the greatest figures in detective fiction, but translated Dante, and created *The Man Born to be King*, as well as 'Guinness is good for you' when she worked at Benson's advertising agency.

So where to next? I thought, the afternoon being young. A visit to St Cedd? The librarian thought it would be muddy. The light was chilled gold; the way was through some of the worst and best of Essex. Grim, 1930s ribbon-development was regularly broken into by beautiful clapboarding, dark steeples, and forest trees.

At last, the Dengie Peninsula and its low farms, and the shimmering North Sea beyond. And there, taller and grander than either of us had remembered, was the Celtic saint's chapel. Once, when I had read poetry in it, seagulls joined in. He had made it out of stones from the Count of the Saxon Shore's bastion against the northern invaders. Coldly sacred, it made us want to pray, if not to kneel.

The last mile was indeed muddy, but the verges were bright emerald springtime grass, and there was this holy beckoning of sanctity, of message. We spoke of Cedd's community, intoxicated by sea-sounds and those of the gospel as they interwove. The saint had voyaged from Lindisfarne to the East Saxons by boat, they said.

We wrote our names in the book. I imagined his little community, curled up in their beehive dwellings, and then curled up below the new grass. I thought I could hear singing.

I thought, too, of Sayers turning from *The Nine Tailors* to translating Dante, by way of a change; for authorship needs variety. And she, like us, would have come 'to the hour that turns back the longing of seafarers and melts their hearts . . . and pierces the new traveller with love if he hears in the distance the bell that seems to measure the dying day'.

So we trudged back to the car, and past homecoming dogs and birds. We thought of compline, of the forlorn count, and of the youthful Cedd, and of all sea-edge people.

On Setting Out

AS FAR as I know, while everything else was drenched in comment, the poet at the wonderful Obama ceremony was not. The BBC commentary was noisy and intrusive, and at one time drowned out the music.

Like the vast audience half-caught in a dream, I suddenly found myself imagining what it would have been like if Emily Dickinson had read at Abraham Lincoln's inauguration in 1861. That was the year a whole torrent of her work included the poem:

> I'm Nobody! Who are you?
> Are you – Nobody – Too?
> Don't tell! they'd advertise – you know!
>
> How dreary – to be – Somebody!
> How public – like a Frog –

To tell one's Name – the livelong June –
To an admiring Bog!

Except she would have been wrong, of course – although salutary in a way both Lincoln and Obama, men of language, would have understood. And that Baptist fervour – how it made us all re-recognize these United States! And the sea of fine black faces – what have we white Christians done to them? The whole business was a vast sermon, one of the greatest ever preached.

Back at the ranch, I went on raking and tidying, coppicing and gathering sticks for all I was worth. 'You can see where you have been!' cried the ramblers. 'So should you,' I felt like saying, being in this sermonic mood. But I laughed and waved.

In the lectionary, Saul is setting out for the blinding light at the Damascus gate, his pocket full of death-warrants. He won't be able to see again until he gets to Straight Street.

The famous conversion makes me think of John Bunyan's allegory – the one that continues to dominate the politics of New England. Bunyan was worried about *Pilgrim's Progress*. Who would take him seriously if he published it? I mean, a tale! Embarrassingly, it became a bestseller, but soon, like any author with a runaway success on his or her hands, he would write:

My pilgrim's book has travelled sea and land . . .
In France and Flanders where men kill each other
My pilgrim is esteemed a friend, a brother . . .
'Tis in New England under such advance . . .
As to be trimmed, new clothed and decked with gems,
That it might show its features, and its limbs,
Yet more; so comely doth my pilgrim walk,
That of him thousands daily sing and talk!

The new administration in Washington is on a pilgrimage, and has said so in eloquent words. The world is at its worst, and in biblical terms: the Gaza massacre, toppling Mammon, melting nature. The youthful Jeremiah in the White House cries to the nation at large, 'Get going! Don't leave it all to me.' An audacious order, as he confessed.

What is Prayer?

PRAYER, we are famously told, is 'something understood'. By a divine poet, no doubt, but not always by me – although its sometimes-mistiness never wholly conceals its reality. Most of us pray publicly in a kind of rain of liturgical sound, and privately in a mostly petitionary silence.

I fancy myself at prayer at about 6 a.m. when, regular as clockwork, I sit for a whole hour with a mug of tea looking at Duncan's hill through a hazel tree. 'You want to cut that down,' he says. 'When John [Nash] lived here, he could paint my furrows.'

The trouble with this argument is that the hazel is at its most prayer-useful in February, the coppicing time; for it is then that its polished branches and glorious catkins entice (George Herbert) both thought and vision. After which, of course, it leafs and constrains them.

The question is, should the hazel go this coming winter, and my prayers no longer be able to filter through its bareness in a quiet and shapely fashion, will the meditative faculty be given a destructive freedom? Perhaps I should sit at 6 a.m. in another chair in another room, and have another view.

On Sunday, I preached on Dr Johnson, who wrote his prayers down. Although he was masterly in his summing up of other men, he was ill-fitted to sum up himself. Mercifully, he had James Boswell to tell him who he was. Thus we have two accounts of him which never quite come together. But then this would happen to most of us. Autobiography and biography may be about the same person, but they are sure to be miles apart.

I think it was Lord Melbourne who said that biography added a new terror to death. I once dreamed that King Henry VIII was sitting on his throne on Tower Hill, eating cold chicken, as Dr Simon Schama, Lady Antonia Fraser, the late Professor Collingwood, and Miss Hilary Mantel were led out to the scaffold, one by one, and beheaded.

Johnson, of course, comes to us in two magnificent versions; his own, with its profound humility, and his friend's. With its genius. He knew that his prayers were as much a part of his existence as his toil and his recreation; so he wrote them down. He never heard God say: 'What nonsense is this, Samuel?'

Thus he wrote:

Let me not linger in ignorance and doubt . . . withdraw my mind from difficulties vainly curious, and doubts impossible to be solved . . . afford me calmness of mind, and steadiness of purpose . . . forgive my presumption . . . feed me with food convenient for me . . . Lord bless me . . . Tomorrow I purpose to regulate my room.

And he prayed, quite uselessly, to be able to get out of bed before noon. Some can; some cannot. And there's an end to it. Not everyone has an overgrown hazel.

Not the least amazing thing about Jesus, him a Temple man, was that he showed that prayer was something that had to be learnt. When his friends saw him at prayer, they said: 'Teach us how to pray.' They who would have followed the Hebrew prayer-patterns of each day. Prayer, it seems, sometimes has to be unlearnt in order to be understood.

There are a positive galaxy of teachers. My tutors have been the unknown author of *The Cloud of Unknowing*, and the poet St John of the Cross. But Dr Johnson, while often denigrating his own prayerfulness, is a mastermind in this area, owing to his inability to see himself as he truly was.

FEBRUARY

Any Other Business

I ALWAYS return from the PCC with the feeling of having said a good many silly things.

Looking back over the years, I see a range of venues, which stretch from frigid church halls to Henry's cosy sitting-room, from hard stack-chairs to his deep sofa. But the denizens are the same, the dear faces, the expected pleas and wraths, the common sense, the amazing abilities, the astonishing methods of raising funds, the hand of strong government.

With ice outside, we arrange garden parties. With snowy boots in the hall and socks on Henry's carpet, we organize the flower festival. This May it will have the theme of the Benedicite, and Alex has drawn the 'O Ananias, Azarias, and Misael, bless ye the Lord; praise him, and magnify him for ever' straw.

I recommend her to see the John Piper window in Aldeburgh Parish Church. I adore this canticle. We sing it in triple verses during Lent, and the liturgical space between ourselves and the Middle Ages vanishes. 'O ye green things upon the earth, bless ye the Lord.'

This green thing makes his usual hopeless suggestions. Barry is practical re the acer that threatens the church porch. Planted by a Victorian priest, it is gradually perishing, and must come down. Not in its present dead-branch-by-dead-branch state, but all at once. There is honey fungus round its roots.

But it and the Saxon tower have lived long enough together for there to be bereavement. But, too, the tree-fellers, taking our grief into consideration, will turn its trunk into planks for the choir vestry. 'And so let us end with the Grace,' says Henry. So let us. And the slide home on black ice.

I am writing a book about my old fields. Up hill and down dale they always were. The poor struggling Suffolk Punches and the one-foot-in-the-furrow ploughman. And the dreadful February draining of the land with faggots, the numb hands, the winter sun tumbling behind the elms. And a far bell tolling a death.

The archaeologists arrive with news of the circus. A few miles east, in Colchester, they have found a Roman circus. Well, not a ring, but 400 yards of stone seating for 15,000 spectators. I can hear their cries as the chariots race. Nothing like this has been discovered in Britain before. We cannot wait to get our spades on it.

These Romans had a little church by the new police station, and, as well as the circus shouts, I hear their hymns. Maybe Prudentius's Cultor Dei, memento.

Servant of God, remember
The stream thy soul bedewing,
The grace that came upon thee
Anointing and renewing.

The Cross dissolves the darkness,
And drives away temptation;
It calms the wavering spirit
By quiet consecration. Amen.

Class Rooms

JOHN calls for me, and we drive a couple of miles to see the latest metamorphosis of our village school. It is raw cold, with bouts of glory in the sky, receding rain, and pure streaks of yellow and blue. The school is where the new Education Act put it in the 1870s. It has two teachers, a secretary, John (the caretaker), and 19 children.

John and I recall our stints as school governors, but everything has changed since then. The air-raid-shelters-cum-rubbish-dumps-cum-loos have become offices, and the Gothic Victorian classrooms have become a space to dance in.

This is where we sat in government, squeezed into infant chairs on long evenings as we ruled the roost. And I, subconsciously recalling that great Second World War poem 'Naming of parts', succumbed to a lifelong failing, and stared out of the window.

Except, now I come to think of it, this would have been nigh impossible, since classroom windows were then set too high to see out of. For the first half-century of the Education Act, 'scholars', as they were called in the register, might be lucky if they caught a glimpse of a cloud. Eighty boys and girls roared the catechism and multiplication tables in this tall room, until the church clock struck four. Then there was a stampede into the muddy fields.

John has pulled up the fitted carpet to reveal cherry-wood herringbone blocks, smoothed of whatever hobnailed boots did to them, and shows their extravagant surface. He possesses, above everything, that gift of knowing at once what is right.

Two new classrooms on a lawn. Eight new walls covered with art. Impressionist ballerinas and gardens. The 19 artists are rather still in the playground, and may be hoping that the break will soon be over; for these are children of warm interiors, of hot cars and sultry homes, and comforting screens. A race unknown to me.

John, the gifted head teacher, and I would have been given cress sandwiches and Tizer on a Saturday and told by mother: 'Off you go. Have a nice time – and don't come in till teatime!' But the children still love reading. Books! The flint and cherry-wood Education Act school went through much grim reading to fit it for farm labouring and domestic service, the trenches, and religion.

Who would have thought that it would emerge into what struck me as a peerless situation for one's first learning? Why on earth do the middle classes in an English village, with primary schools like this, pay for private education? It, and proper teaching at home, could be as durable as the unexpected parquet. But I can see OFSTED fainting.

Someone on the radio is inexpertly describing the education of Jesus. It must have been remarkable, if perhaps unorthodox. Was he not constantly addressed as 'Rabbi'? And that intellectual spirit – how it burst through the frowsty legalism and so-called learnedness of his day! And, most of all, that literary brilliance, the poetry and short stories! 'Where did he get it from?' they said. Where did he? From the enchanting library of the old covenant, and from watching and listening and thinking, mostly outside. We see him write only once, and that with his finger in dust.

Captain Brown

IN THE BITTER February churchyard the dead retell their tales as I pass. It is bitter cold. Maybe it is the fat snowflakes that throw Gordon's story out of season. The little Lancs captain, having marched all through the Western Desert, is now part of the Control Commission in Germany. The Colonel cannot wait to get the regimental silver out for Christmas. It will be grace, and the loyal toast, and all the trimmings – mess dress and all. We'll show them!

There are fat snowflakes. They fall on a flattened town. The concentration camps have been discovered; so there is no pity. No pity at all. Christmas dinner is laid out in a long glass orangery, which, strangely, has not been shattered.

The band plays. The turkeys are carved. The food is mountains high. But watchers and the holy ones press their angelic faces to the panes outside. The officers are not hungry. The band sways about. The Colonel says: 'They've got it coming to them.' Then sends for more plates. The starving children eat, then sing.

By a sequence of unplanned moves, the captain arrives in our village to be our churchwarden – for ages. There is his grave, by the hedge. In his 90th year, he had some whisky, went to his four-poster bed, and went to God. And now he is telling his tale out of turn. It must be the wild snow. What else?

I rake sticks, etc., out of the snowdrop bank and listen to geese going over. David Holt comes to stay. Early on Sunday morning – Lent 1 – I listened to him reading a poem on *Something Understood* with the Chief Rabbi. That good programme. The wind shouts and howls in the naked trees.

I preach on the desert. Severely. Not many in church, but

great beauty. And the first aconites. Branches whack the air. John and Meriel take me home in their 4×4, sploshing down my farm track, getting muddy, being thoughtful. She has been reading Barack Obama, that remarkable writer. I am reading Chekhov. I think of the Lord's desolation, the stoniness, the loneliness, his terrible way ahead. 'Lord Jesus, think on me,' we sang in the chilly aisles. The white cat dreams.

After lunch, I write some more of my book. Nobody calls either at the door or on the phone. I say compline before going to bed, only it should be a duet: a plea and its response. And all the things that go bump in the night have stopped prowling around like a roaring lion seeking someone to devour – though keep us tonight, Lord. Fast means keep.

Once upon a time, farm labourers turned on hay-bales above my head, wishing the night twice as long, reaching their prickly beds by ladder – though feathers for the farmer and his wife. No hot-water bottle, no *Something Understood* of a Sunday. Matins for the missus, evensong for her servants. And bait for the horses. And parson going on and on. And Satan vexing sore, as well he might. But now this quiet house. No shoals of shouting boys and girls, no cattle lowing. Just the crack of a stiffening beam and the tap of a barren rose on the window. To think it would have come to this!

Most things done, I plant my wild sweetpea seeds from Tuscany in Tom Thumb pots, two at a time. I can already smell their heavy southern scent. Who brought them here?

Walking the Tithe Map

A DAY OF indescribably wonderful winter loveliness. I must say something about it, however, as the sun is hot on my neck. I am sitting, of course, with my back to the window, as this is the creative position. To face February full on, with the last snow being pulled from the grass like a rug, would be destructive to all other thought. Inseparable magpies will be bouncing around an old chopped-up marrow.

A few miles away, in the Castle Park, snow is also being heat-rolled from Roman mosaic floors and corporation pavements. A hare sits still on the exposed barn floor. The white cat roasts in the kitchen window. The postman arrives. Having read in the newspapers that there are icebergs, ten-feet drifts, etc. once you get off the main road, he has walked down the track. I thank him profusely. Film-makers then appear to get some snow-shots to accompany my snow-reading. Hurry, hurry! Winter is running away before your very eyes.

I telephone the hymns for matins. It is the feast of St Scholastica, but I keep them simple. She was St Benedict's twin sister. She wanted him to sit up all night to discuss the delights of heaven, but he refused. Thereupon she prayed for dreadful weather, and something even worse than any forecaster can invent roared around Monte Cassino, and he had to stay.

She had the brains; he had the organization. They share a grave. A dreadful battle would one day shake their clever bones.

A pair of blanketed horses nose the snow away as they graze. My bamboo is Chinese, faintly rattling in the breeze and being intrusive as ever. A caller, dressed for a Captain Scott expedition, begs a bit of it. It would be a good time to walk the Tithe Map for a book I am writing, I decide. The Map is signed

'Roger Kynaston'. It is May 1844 – the Hungry Forties – and no good time for tithes.

The poor would be gathering sticks to boil a pot; the better sort would be, well, hoping for the best. The village school would be intoning tables and collects. The vicar would be reading *The* (free to the clergy) *Times*. The church would possess its medieval clerestory for a few more years.

What did the Victorian restorers do with all that ancient building material? I expect to find fragments of it bodged into a farm wall, but I never do. How confident they were – to take down a clerestory and to put up a (very good) wooden roof. And all that glass . . . But I must not go on. That way lies madness.

I must live today. It is what February insists. It says: 'Make your own report on the winter.' Think of curates like Francis Kilvert. He didn't stay in. He strode across the Black Mountains, calling out to the housekeeper, 'I'll be back for supper!'

I am making this up in order to get myself into a proper frame of mind for attending the Friends of St Andrew's committee meeting tonight. For it will be bitter-dark then, and nearly as bad as one is told by the weathermen. Tom's reservoir will be wearing its thin black skin of ice. Pheasants will scuttle sadly as I pass.

Perhaps, when the sun goes in, I will ring Tom and plead terrible illness. The time will come when the night will be as seductive as the day, and no one can stay in, and the telly will grow moss.

MARCH

Ruins

A SOFT DAY. The temperature has crawled up several degrees. Soundless rain. Six primroses and thousands of snowdrops drink in the pleasure of it. Wet blackbirds squabble for rotting D'Arcy Spice apples. All being well, I shall clear the long walk of its blackened leaves.

Richard has cleared the tottering garage, leaving a new view. The defunct white goods, as the shops call them, have been taken to the dump, plus the stone-age telly, and other things that have been in hiding. A sulky bonfire has gradually reduced all that is reducible to pale ashes.

Richard's mother arrives with Harry, aged six. We sit in the old farm kitchen, drinking coffee, and between us we bring back the voices it has listened to for centuries. Not Harry, of course, who is sworn to speechlessness, and who buries his head in his grandmother's side. A chocolate unburies him for a minute.

After they have gone, I revel in the unexpected extent of the new view and Richard's neatness, and stand by the dwindling pyre. Black horse-pond water has now become cloud-mirroring horse-pond water. The bent quince will have to learn how to stand up straight. The garage was a Second World War construction, with massive doors from, possibly, a Civil War barn, and when their ashes are cold I will rake out their vast hinges.

I have sent my John Clare book to the publisher, and he too has left a visionary space. It is quite hard for a writer to begin all over again. To loaf. Or to find a title for the book that is in the post. Clare's dilemma was to find paper, not titles. Much of his archive, which was huge, was written on old scraps. No matter. Students from universities bring me immaculate pages, their words on one side only. What Clare would have given for their blank reverse!

Once, he thought he had found an answer to the paper shortage in the form of the dried-out under-bark of a tree. He tried it out with his goose quill, and the letters neither stuck nor ran. Often, he did not bother with titles, and called poem after poem 'Song'. He once claimed 'A right to song'.

Christchurch topples as I type. A young man during the lunch hour watches its cathedral spire waver and fall into the street. It was raised on a fault, as was all that beautiful city.

Each March, the East Anglian Readers spend a day at Selwyn College, Cambridge. Church of England Readers are curiously isolated people, but this annual getting together does wonders. At the violin-led service in chapel, I find myself pondering on George Selwyn, whose portrait hangs above High Table, and who was made Missionary Bishop of New Zealand in 1841. He was 42.

They said he taught himself the Maori language on the ship. They also said that he was 'a Tractarian in his convictions', whose formal protest against a clause in the Civil Letter Patent, professing to 'give him power to ordain', signalled the beginnings of a new Erastian conception of the Colonial Episcopate. This year, the Archbishop of York, Dr Sentamu, will

be with us at Selwyn College, in a reversal of colonial epis-
copacy.

This Readers' outing has been a gift to us by my friend John
Wood, and is about 20 years old. Do other parts of the country
have one? If not, they should. But tragic New Zealand, with its
fault-lines hidden from the Victorian Church . . .

Who is Counting?

THE SPRING arrived on Monday. Thousands of snowdrops in
my wood, which had hung there in a closed, waiting state,
opened up. Birdsong became loud and bell-like. There was an
exultant calling from bare trees. Even the men prodding about
in the squishy mess that was supposed to be the lower cart-
track, searching for a leakage, sounded joyful. They raised their
voices in childlike delight when the water level began to rise
around their wellies. 'We've found the spring!' they cried.

I turned off the radio. It has been running money, money,
money without stop. I was born when farmers hadn't two
pennies to rub together, as they said. This was bad. But isn't it
equally bad to have millions of pounds to rub along with? To
pile up this when one is old, as the rich men's faces on the screen
frequently are? Who is counting? Everybody, it seems.
Eventually, the total becomes astronomical, and pointless even
to Mr Peston; for all I see are his wide eyes as the figures stretch
them beyond comprehension.

In the old manor house on its Saxon mound (to prevent the
Stour from seeping in) we discuss the parish's future. The
young are dubious, the old philosophical. It was here before
Domesday, and how can it not be here after Madoff, as it were?

Of course, the village bodger and not the diocesan architect kept the church more or less watertight. The books showed the care and expense. 'Mr Smith, for mending the tower, £3.'

Young men straight from the commuters' train and still in their smart suits tot up what we have and what may be required of us. Stone window-frames made in 1450 need repairing. They must have accepted the lowest estimate. George Herbert used to say, 'Nothing lasts but the Church!' To his mother's horror, he paid for the rebuilding of Bemerton and Leighton Bromswold out of his own pocket, the latter as an architectural version of his poetry.

After the meeting, Tom and I talk about his herd of Lincolns and how very soon – well, April – he will open the shed doors, and, after a moment of disbelief at such good fortune, these cows will rush out of prison into the water-meadows, leaping and bellowing with bliss.

Tom loves his animals too much for his own comfort. He gives them names, which they say is a mistake. A heifer to the slaughter is one thing; Kevin to the slaughter, another.

Me: 'You haven't got a bullock named Kevin?'

Tom's wife: 'Yes, he had.'

Alas, poor Kevin. Alas, poor Tom. I tell the white cat, 'Your name is Kitty.' She looks amazed.

At night, the ancient rooms say, 'It will soon be Lent.' All day, I write my Tithe Map book, only breaking off for reccies round what used to be my fields, getting cold and muddy.

Having to help judge a literary prize, I read, read, and read. The authors are all strange to me, as indeed are some of their publishers. There was a time when it was all familiar, the names, the colophons on the spines, the puffs on the backs. In a way it is refreshing – and an education.

I read the obituary of Edward Upward, died aged 105, whose life contained all my youthful reading and all 20th-century politics, all its ideals and rebellion. All of its excellent literary style.

Between Rooms

IN THE NOVEL that I read and re-read as the priming-the-pump exercise for the day's work ahead, poor Albertine tells her lover: 'To think that I shall never see this room again, these books, that pianola, the whole house, I cannot believe it and yet it is true.' The relationship has foundered on distrust.

But her farewell to her room is a reminder to us all of the loss of a room when its owner, a friend of many years, dies – goes to what the old translator called one of the Father's many mansions. Thereupon the room in which we sat and talked for half a lifetime is stripped and sold and is no more.

This death of a beloved room occurred to me, once in the village, once in Cambridge; and, like Albertine, I think, 'That clutter of objects, that mandolin-strumming lad under his glass dome, my winged chair, those good and bad pictures, I shall never see them again, how strange and yet it is true.'

In the old people's home there can be a favourite piece of furniture from the real home. It is permitted. On the telly, the characters in the soaps wrangle and fornicate in rooms that would be as familiar to the old eyes as the ones she has left.

Pot plants fight for life above the radiator. Beautiful young attendants of either sex tap and enter with cups of weak tea. From Indonesia? They smile. They miss family, not rooms. The loss of rooms comes later.

It then occurs to me, quite suddenly, like a bout of common sense, that the person I have come to see, and who is in her nineties, is so advanced in what might be called room-consciousness that her pretty drawing room has long vanished, and this alarmingly expensive room in the old people's home, too, is on the way out, as one might say. And that she is between accommodations, so to speak, and somehow happily so.

But not so far gone heavenwards as to forget her always perfect earthly manners. 'I have some Chablis in the fridge,' she tells the nurse. He returns and pours us each half a glass. 'Cheers, darling,' she says to him. She cannot see to read, her radio doesn't work, and the telly is a blank. There are no hours in the day and no days in the week. She is with me, and yet beyond me. It is as it is in great old age.

Back home, the clocks go forward – I think, I am never quite sure. I get up at six and drink good strong Yorkshire tea (a present) from an L. S. Lowry mug and watch the harsh March sunlight streak through the hazels. The house is due east with a big hill protecting it. The horses have lost their blankets, and their coats shine. A pair of red-legged partridges, a devoted couple, are politely gobbling up the rotten apples.

The furniture sits where it has sat for ages. The interior-designer friend used to move it around – in his head, that is, for neither I nor his other hosts ever took his advice. He'd put the table there, and 'throw out those curtains'. Time and time again, over the centuries, this room would have been emptied, refilled, reordered, but only now would one person fill it.

The table legs show much children's kicking with country boots. Presumably the Nazareth house would have contained good furniture? And then the poor homeless Lord.

The Tower Captain Dies

MARKET DAY in the small Suffolk town. Brilliant March sunshine. Three times as many stalls as in my boyhood, and many times less noise. Instead of shouting and entertaining, the stallholders quietly cower below their awnings. Where do they all come from? Where do they disappear to? The great artist Thomas Gainsborough, a native lad, looks down on them from his plinth, brush in hand.

I visit a friend in the retirement home, where a cheerful soul asks if I can manage the stairs, compliments me on my 'healthy face', and tells me, 'We have three Maggies.' In the hot bedroom, my dear Maggie and I drink a little Chablis, and gossip. Say what you like, the retirement home is a strange business. Stay at home if you can. A few yards away, the River Stour shimmers coldly, and the oak buds fatten. A few yards away, all is as it was.

But not the town itself. The faint howl of the sawmill, the thump and splash of the flourmill, the rich reek of the maltings, the marvellous scent of the numerous family bakers and that of many other back-shop trades, the musk and ring of the blacksmith's forge, the piteous cries coming from the cattle market are no more. But the celebrated Suffolk silk-weavers flourish. Thus this recessional quiet.

The local TV channel talks of unemployment. The country buses weave through the ancient streets like gaudy whales, and the car parks are bursting. Waitrose says: 'Let us take you away from all this.' I take a rest in an unchanged old pub, and watch a different world go by.

Bernard has died. He was our life vice-president of the Essex Association of Change Ringers, and many other great things.

He said the office for belfry use, which begins with: 'Praise him upon the well-tuned cymbals. Praise him upon the loud cymbals.' He carried the processional cross before me at matins. He had what is known as 'presence', and just seeing him unlooping his rope in the tower brought stability to the service.

His spiritual home was the lovely church of St-Leonard-at-the-Hythe in Colchester, whose 1985 redundancy brought him to us; and what a gift!

And now he is gone. The Church of England has its true servants, its confident artists, men and women who know its ways, odd though they might seem to some. Last summer, Bernard sat in my garden, looking not quite himself, while his friends gathered greenery for a wedding.

It was he who must have made me an honorary ringer, though I have never pulled a rope. My contribution has been to provide a bit of bell-history, although I am pretty certain that Bernard knew it all.

How shall we honour his passing? With what quarter peal? Who will now carry the psalm, the Benedicite in a thin congregation? He was the Master of the association, its property trustee, and a dozen other things. He rang in all the cathedrals. And when he took the chair after our annual ringers' evensong, it was like the arrival of someone in authority, the chatter dying away, the respect mounting.

It was through him that I entered the esoteric world of bell-founding and -casting, handbells, and all the successors of Stedman's bell tunes.

Benedicite

TWO MIGHTY songs this week: the Benedicite, and the nightingale's – the latter on tape, for the singer is not yet due. But they disturb the universe. Each year I say the same thing: 'We now have the Benedicite instead of the Te Deum, because it is springtime as well as Lent,' and off we go, 'Praise him and magnify him for ever!'

No cuts and no nightingales, unless we include them in 'All ye fowls of the air'. But otherwise a pretty full litany of nature. And with 'Ye spirits and souls of the righteous', departed congregations join in.

It is what the holy children sang to Nebuchadnezzar from the fire, and what Christians have sung from the earliest times; an earthy as well as a celestial song, which St Francis might well have had in mind when, in 1225, he sat in the garden of San Damiano at Assisi and wrote his 'Canticle of the Sun'. 'Be thou praised, my Lord, with all thy creatures, above all Brother Sun.'

And the March sun makes Aldeburgh glitter as we fill the Jubilee Hall for Richard Mabey's lecture on 'The Barley Bird', i.e. the nightingale. He and I would sometimes listen to it at Tiger Hill, where I heard it as a boy; the long, operatic thread of notes from the hidden performer, the disturbed woodland, the silenced humanity.

At the ancient farmhouse, it would sing against the rattle of my push-mower, dazzling music as an accompaniment to its clackety-clack. And so filled with nightingales was Suffolk in those days that boots would be hurled at them from bedroom windows, so that weary labourers could get a mite of sleep. Yet it remained a fugitive bird. If we had the full song, we never had the singer. It took a great poet to creep up on him and see its unassuming source. John Clare would find him 'lost in a wilderness of listening leaves'.

Vicky and I wander round Aldeburgh, and observe the sea slapping the shingle. Apart from lecture folk, there is no one about. The hard Victorian buildings are scrubbed for the season, the big gulls shouting on the rooftops. An Alfred Wallis boat balances on the horizon. The little pub where I used to read and write is empty. The sky is pale blue, the water navy-blue. Maggi Hambling's shells are white and far away; Benjamin Britten's house red and near; the churchyard full of Children of Men and Priests of the Lord; the hotels full of Servants of the Lord warming up the rooms, one hopes.

Back home, the Flower Festival committee meets, its theme this year being – the Benedicite. One parish has a theme, the other does not, simply piling the blooms around. It is ingenuity and/or profusion, to avoid competition. O all ye Green Things upon the earth.

Back home, book proofs have arrived, and must be read with a fine-tooth comb lest some terrible word gets into print. The white cat and I check them with diligence, although she cannot spell. Animals like to find us at some mechanical task, breathing regularly, set in our ways. These are essays written long ago, so that I keep running into my previous self, sometimes with admiration, though not always.

Did the author of the Benedicite run through his list thinking, 'Have I left something out? Yes, whales.' Was the song a spontaneous invention by all three Children, verse after verse? Did crazy Nebuchadnezzar join in? Who couldn't? Did they all hear Mesopotamian nightingales?

St John of the Cross

AT THE MOMENT, the desert could not be more with us, and properly so, since it is Lent. The three mighty Abrahamic faiths, which were bred in the desert, lay down their distinctive rules. Dr Jacobs, from Berlin, who is here for the weekend, says the Kaddish for the sabbath before we have dinner.

The Hebrew words float across the ancient room, while, at near-midnight, I go to the study to put together something for Sunday matins. In between, names such as Benghazi on the radio remind me of a favourite poet from the Second World War, Sidney Keyes, who died in the Western Desert just before his 21st birthday; and also of Monty and Rommel, and of the Roman coin on the mantelpiece which someone found in the Libyan sand.

And now a mud desert in Japan. Silence, not words, for this in our petitionary prayers. And most decidedly no God's-will-versus-tectonic-plates sermon.

Thus, I ramble a little about St John of the Cross, whose papers were saved from destruction by the South African poet Roy Campbell. The desert was where people went for a bit of quiet – for the riches of solitude. St John was a small, humble man who did not think of himself as a poet at all. His Christ was the Bridegroom of the Gospels, which made him the bride. It was all very Spanish.

A woman had told him that her prayer was about 'Considering the beauty of God, and in rejoicing that he possessed such beauty'. When St John heard this, he knew that he had found the imagery for his poetry. It was that of the seeking lover – the seeking lover of both sides. Christ sought him as eagerly as he sought Christ. The landscape in which they sought each other was that of wild rocky Toledo. And, should you go there, and with some knowledge of the saint's poetry, these solitudes will feed you as satisfyingly as the spaciousness of a cathedral.

When I stayed in Westminster Deanery with my friends Michael and Alison Mayne, we sometimes walked at midnight through the Abbey. Just a little light here and there. Plantaganets gleaming, their hands stiff with prayer, black windows, black slabs in Poets' Corner, ravishing angels aloft, white nobodies on plinths, lovely distances, a trapped holiness, and not a soul in sight.

John Clare sharing a wall with Matthew Arnold, Geoffrey Chaucer sharing a language with us all. The Unknown Soldier ebony deep, his artificial flowers blackest of all. 'Look,' Michael says, 'Anne of Cleves.' They said that Anne and Henry VIII played cards on their wedding night, which was one way of passing the time: Henry almost fainted when he saw her.

But back to the desert, and St John of the Cross, who was not popular. They said he worked too hard, and that he was a crony (disciple) of the quite overwhelming St Teresa of Avila. And that he could be very accusing when he liked. They put him in prison, but he remained unconfined; so it was all a waste of time.

His favourite outdoor spot was by the River Guadalimar, where he heard 'The music without sound, The solitude that clamours,' and was nourished by 'The supper that revives us and enamours.'

The Initiates

THE SUCCESSIVE nature of plant sites. When did not celandine patch the same foot or two of ditch-bank along the Little Horkesley Road? The school bus lurches by, just missing it. Today's mostly car-bound villages have no knowledge of it. But there it is, in its territorial gold-leaf, shining and perfect. And on the second day of spring. The machine that cut a rain-grig last week just missed it.

The air is soft and scented; the sun has some heat in it. They said that my Lesser Celandine was called 'Swallow herb' because 'it beginneth to springe and to flowre at the coming of the swallows.' They also said that it was called figwort (fig piles) for another reason. It knows nothing of this, only that it blooms in this place.

The tall bishop leans down as the little boy confirms what his godparents said only seven years ago, and makes a cross on his snowy forehead. 'Samuel.'

There are other confirmings. I read from Romans a few paragraphs of the gospel according to Paul. They are complex. They fly around the nave, and probably in one ear and out of the other. The candidates sip from the ancient cup, Samuel like a little bird. We all sing 'Lead me all my journey through', and 'Feed me till I want no more'. There is a hint of cakes and tea.

I am reading *The Cloud of Unknowing*, an anonymous masterpiece of the 14th century by an English author. It was quite common at the time for people not to put their names to anything – 'God knows my name.' The Penguin Classics translation is by Clifton Wolters, a man to whom we are in debt for his being able to admit us to the powerful glories of the late-medieval world. Take the following:

36

St Luke tells us that when our Lord was in the house of Martha, her sister . . . Mary sat at his feet. And as she listened to him she regarded neither her sister's busy-ness (and it was a good and holy business; is it not the first part of the active life?), nor his priceless and blessed physical perfection, nor the beauty of his human voice and words (and this is an advance, for this is the second part of the active life, as well as the first part of the contemplative). But what she was looking at was the supreme wisdom of his Godhead shrouded by the words of his humanity.

And on this she gazed with all the love of her heart. Nothing she saw or heard could budge her, but there she sat, completely still, with deep delight, and an urgent love eagerly reaching out into that high cloud of unknowing that was between her and God.

I want to say this: no one in this life, however pure, and however enraptured with contemplating and loving God, is ever without this intervening, high, and wonderful cloud. It was in this same cloud that Mary experienced the many secret movements of her love. Why? Because this is the highest and holiest state of contemplation we can know on earth.

Anonymity is now the least thing that we desire. No sooner do we 'see' what must be 'beyond' us, than we set to work to explain it. 'And a cloud took him from their sight.' The author of *The Cloud of Unknowing*, however, exonerates poor Martha from being practical when she should have been staring.

Libraries

IS IT NOT a fact that when a bookcase is emptied out upon the floor its contents double in volume? Such tall unsteady piles. I sit among them, regretting my folly. It was the local-history bookcase, and Suffolk had wandered up into Norfolk, and Essex into the Soke of Ely. I thought a clean sweep was demanded.

Long ago, when I was a youth, I was sent to convey Canon Gerald Rendall's library from his big old house to the local museum, to which he had generously bequeathed it. He had been a mighty scholar, although, in spite of this, he had believed that Lord Oxford was Shakespeare. None the less, he had a fine library, and it was a splendid gift to the borough. Also, I had been given his school prize for mathematics, Boswell's *Life of Samuel Johnson*, still a treasure, which, though massive, I had carried all around the Hebrides on one of those 'in the steps of' journeys.

But back to the Canon's house, where his conifers rattled against the windows in a kind of mourning. The library window was wide, and a truck was parked below it, and down to it the removal men were sliding his precious books like coals. They were making a start, they said, whistling cheerfully. Beautiful bindings with his crest, fluttering pages, first editions fell from the duckboard in a heap.

Shock must have lent my voice authority; for the removal men's carnage came to a sudden halt. As I was putting the already trucked books into some kind of decent order, I heard one of them say: 'You know I don't mind what I do, Bob, but I hate moving a parson – half a ton of bloody books before you start.'

Outside my window – I am in my house now – the pre-Easter

gale blows. It is the kind of wild weather that I once found bliss-
ful and inviting. 'Come and join us!' it would howl. Jean's
horses prance about as if in a circus, their manes waving. Spring
grass, which wasn't there yesterday, ripples. 'Come outside!'
shrieks the wind. 'Get bashed about like the birds and the trees.'
Get pneumonia, more like, says my ancient self. But the rain-
filled clouds remain enticing, and the noise of the weather stays
thrilling.

I possess one book-lined room that I hesitate to call the
library. Else it is tottering bookcase after bookcase all over the
house, its floors being up hill and down dale, so that each of
them has to be wedged steady. Never again will I tip them out,
but sort them on the shelf.

For Jane Austen, the library was a male sanctuary. Ladies read
on sofas or while making gooseberry jam. Anywhere. Men were
delicate creatures who had to have a refuge from their
tiresomeness. Mr Bennet would clearly have become insane
without his library, his safe door against silly women.

What did Mr Bennet read? Not novels, one thinks. Or, nearly
as fictitious, the Baronetage. I think Boswell's *Life of Samuel
Johnson* as he imagined swapping Mrs Bennet for the Hebrides.
His book-fed calm drives her up the wall, if one may be vulgar.
But, like a sensible parent, he sees that what might be called book
sanity takes root in one child – Elizabeth. So maybe she and her
lovely husband will read together, laughing, pages turning in
unison – which, to my mind, is part of a desirable marriage.

There was an American who said: 'They tell me life is the
thing, but I prefer reading.' But this can't be right, tempting
though it is.

An Outing

'FOR, LO, the winter is past, the rain is over and gone; the flowers appear on the earth, the time of the singing of birds is come . . .' This is what I had had carved on the tomb of the artist John Nash. Lichen is gradually erasing it, but it is literally true at this moment. What a cold rainy winter it has been. What a singing of birds it is. What a sun pours into the garden and against the old walls, now that the hazel coppicing has been done.

And here is the Song of Solomon open on my desk. 'Make haste, my beloved' urges the last verse. 'How beautiful are thy feet . . .', but I mustn't go on. Scholars scratch their heads over its origin and say that if it is not read allegorically it has no business being included in the canon. But writers I love – St John of the Cross, Richard Rolle, St Teresa of Avila – loved it; so I love it too. And my singing birds break off to feed on chopped apples and mouldy Christmas cake. What a blessing it is when something cannot be certain.

To be correct, the singing of the chainsaw has come and gone. David brought down a mighty aspen bough which was drawing up the kitchen garden to fruitless heights. Its logs will dry out for a year, then burn well. But I will miss its dreamy voice, which said: 'Don't do a thing. Let me entrance you.'

Duncan has fished a hefty lump of iron from the horse pond. It was a wheel-brake for a carriage, but now it is corroded into a kind of tuning-fork from Mervyn Peake's *Gormenghast*. There would have been few steep-enough hills around here to need it. Our lanes were notoriously dreadful, and shook carts and carriages to bits.

Lent plods on. I fill it with the humdrum: page-proofs, and raking. I make plans, make unlikely dishes from the turned-out fridge, listen to Gerald Finzi, write kindly refusals, discuss Shakespeare with the white cat, give morning hymns to Meriel, feed the woodman, talk about the water supply with the council officer, and find primroses.

I hear the politicians shouting the odds, and the village football team distantly hollering. All noise is off. A dear friend goes to God at a mighty age, and on the radio Chopin at no age at all. On Saturday, we are off to Cambridge for the annual Readers' conference at Selwyn College.

For 20 or more years, Canon John Woods had drawn the East Anglian Readers there out of our isolation, because, although next-door to each other in our clear landscape, we would not otherwise see each other. Writers who are Readers are doubly locked away, and so I find this jaunt doubly interesting. And I like this budding Cambridge, with the Victorian shrubberies about to burst, and the river damps promising glories along the Backs.

This year, I will say compline at tea-time. And say to people I have met once a year for ages, 'I'm sorry, but I have forgotten your name.' And they will point to their badge, and I will get out my glasses. And George Selwyn will look down from his frame, and so will his son, John, and the undergraduates will look like children. And the drive back to the parish will not be without melancholy. Like a day at the seaside when we were ten.

Lectures are inclined to make me daydream. While some take notes, I take the opportunity to take stock of the days.

Fortune-Hunting

I FIND myself thinking of Jane Austen. She did so like 'nice muggy weather'. Birds wheel indistinctly in the bare trees, and the white barn swims in the near distance. I think of her tomb in Winchester Cathedral. No mention of her novels, of course; only that she was against Enthusiasm in Religion. Her sailor brother was known as 'the officer who knelt in church'. Such fragments tell volumes.

Her characters move against a weather that would sometimes reach the exactitude of today's forecaster. Poor weather turns them into moles, snow makes them panic, heat makes them rude, but nice muggy weather – well!

As for her clergy: handsome Mr Elton never mentions Christ, only rectories; and thick Mr Collins mostly mentions only Lady Catherine; so no wonder Austen herself was reprimanded for her picture of the Church of England.

Death has its virtues. 'What a blessing it is when undue influence does not survive the grave,' Mrs Weston says. Yet all the novels depend on a kind of distilled morality drawn from the quiet practice of Christianity.

Money, too, got Austen into trouble. She had precious little herself. Her heroines might possess small means, but these would attract penniless suitors, for the Married Women's Property Act lay far into the future.

The moment an Austen bride left the altar, her husband took all. This Act has ruined fiction. Sir Walter Scott deplored her mercenary view of marriage but, as she said, while it was wrong to marry for money, it was foolish to marry without it.

Her publisher, John Murray, attempted to purchase the

copyright of *Sense and Sensibility*, *Mansfield Park*, and *Emma* all for £450, and this when she was famous. Although £450 was much more then than it is now, it was a wretched sum.

The vulgar Mrs Elton was allowed to have 'so many thousands as would always be called ten'. Had he succeeded in wooing Miss Woodhouse, Mr Elton would have taken her £30,000, a vast dowry. These figures juggled through my head as I cooked breakfast and listened to the latest economics from the Coalition. In time, will Martin Amis novelize them? Will a later Walter Greenwood write their effect on the poor?

Tom has gone off to buy a cedar. He is planting a wood and is excited and happy. In Austen's day, cedars for English country parks were fetched from Lebanon itself. Ours, in Wormingford churchyard, crashed to the ground in the great gale of 1987. It had risen from a mere plate of roots which, when it was turned on its edge, was like lifting the lid of human mortality.

Countless ivory fragments of villagers lay a foot or so from view. We gathered them up and laid them deep, sawed the cedar, left a dent in the grass. 'You wouldn't know it had been there,' we said. Or ourselves. This is how it will be. In Winchester Cathedral, our greatest novelist and our Saxon princes merge their dust. Unenthusiastically, naturally.

In Psalm 29, God shows his power by bringing cedars to the ground, not brutally but rather as a boy cheerfully knocks down tall plants in a meadow. 'The voice of the Lord breaketh the cedar trees, yea, the Lord breaketh the cedars of Libanus.' The psalm is a heady confusion of destruction and music. Creation tips and sings.

The Bay-Tree and the Desert

THE VAST bay-tree (Laurus nobilis), some 50 feet high, which has stood scented sentinel for so long is dying – I think. Or it is having a spring autumn. Its leaves shrivel on the bough. 'I have seen the wicked in great power, spreading himself like a green bay tree.'

What is happening may not be terminal, however, and if Richard cuts it to the ground it will flourish all over again. Perfumed logs will spark in the grate for winters to come. Hissing and crackling through its fallen leaves, I remember that they should be crowning a poet's brow. This is no way to perish, and all over the primroses as well.

Lent jogs on. Lots of desert news. I am writing the foreword to a book about Virginia Woolf's holidays. Heavens, what undertakings! Half a train-full of hefty luggage, bicycles, and servants. Excursions in all weathers. And, most interestingly, a careful avoidance of all geographic, architectural, and 'general' facts.

Thus the tall novelist could move across England in a kind of personal haziness about this and that, particularly when it came to cathedrals or Stonehenge, or where one would expect a strong reaction, or at least a little wonder.

Sometimes, she is on her own, her bag filled with review copies for *The Times Literary Supplement*, for no Bloomsbury ever stops working, least of all during a holiday; and sometimes she is with Leonard and Vanessa, or five other people, and each day she gives the countryside attributions that one would never find in guidebooks, but which create such perfect settings for the talk in her novels.

Now and then she is ill and strange, and landscape comes to

the rescue. There is a mighty discomfort in these travels, and a kind of pre-Betjeman anger towards those who are getting out of dreadful Victorian cities and into red-brick villas, which were going up wherever their owners fancied; for there was little or no planning.

All the same, it is odd for us highly factualized sightseers to find Virginia's view of Stonehenge labelled, moodily, 'The singular & intoxicating charm . . . is that no one in the world can tell you anything about it . . . I felt as though I had run against the stark remains of an age I cannot otherwise conceive . . . a piece of wreckage washed up from Oblivion.'

No one in our world is disallowed information on anything. 'Oblivion' won't do. But it does do in those perfect novels. In fact, it has to. Indeed, it was sought for in that lonely walk to the river in 1941.

At first, the desert did its utmost to obscure what Christ went to it to find. Its sheer dullness robbed him of his intellect, when it should have cleared it. It weakened his young body; it made horrible sounds. And maybe it did so to the many other seekers after enlightenment who came to it in springtime, as well as to the Desert Fathers, who set up house in it later on.

What the Lord and his followers had to face was Oblivion, and the desert maddeningly waved this possibility in their faces. It was no help. Environmentalists now cause it to say wonderful things. To which the sands can reply: 'Out of us grew the triple Abrahamic faiths of your salvation.'

APRIL

The Saltings

AN APRIL heatwave burns the primroses, and we try out the new garden chairs. A slender horse with snowy fetlocks feeds on new grass. I break off non-toiling to listen to an Ada Leverson story on the radio and, as always, I regret its being dramatized. Novels are not plays.

We discuss the art of reading aloud. David is reading the four Gospels aloud on an audio book. The recording takes place not in my tumultuous garden, with the birds in full cry, but in a Hackney studio. He has planted the potatoes, got the mower to go, and let in the light where willows hogged the sun.

'What is "below the salt?" he enquires. Jesus advises us to take the lowest place when we sit at table, so that our host can say, 'Friend, go up more!' Sitting above or below the salt cellar, a little ditch carved across a medieval table, prevented such solecisms as not knowing one's place.

Later, weeding in the full Lenten sun, the nesting birds still at it, and David deep in St John's Gospel in Hackney, I think of salt and of Kay de Brisay. Her son, Michael, and I sat in the reference library, he reading for the priesthood, myself for no obvious purpose, as became a future writer. His mother delighted me by what I can only call her grandeur, the rash

46

lipstick, the loud voice, the learning (she was an archaeologist) and the cigarettes. And she had written a paper on salt.

I brought it out into the garden and re-read it. 'With all thy offerings thou shalt offer salt' – Leviticus. Hence, Joachim's sprinkling of salt from my cellar when he says Kaddish on Friday nights.

But back to Mrs de Brisay, as I properly called her, and her fascinating paper 'The Red Hills of Essex'. These hills are made of the pottery and briquetage left behind by the salt industry on the Essex marshes. Kay, I mean Mrs de Brisay, says that there are 175 of them strewn from just below Harwich to just above the Thames. They would have been ancient when St Cedd wandered through them, holding the Gospels high above his head. They are the first industrial waste of Essex. Plastics would follow, but in good time.

Brine was heated in clay pots and crystallized into salt. The pots were not reused, hence the pottery hills. And there were clay evaporation tanks where the sea was inned, and let out, leaving its salt behind. Mrs de Brisay and her team dug away in this salt world for four years in the 1970s, her cigarette ash flecking the Iron, Belgic, and Romano-British Ages, her brain at full strength and, I suspected, her happiness complete.

She once took Michael and myself and his sister on to Southend Pier for a treat, sailing along, the wind in her face, breathing in the brine, the colourful scene, making us pause to watch the waves through the cracks.

At Peldon – where the salt dig was – she noted that all the pots were finger-tipped. Peldon was entirely Iron Age. They found the bones of a young man, else it was all pots. Potten Island glimmered out to sea. All sodium chloride, it was.

You can still buy it, and usually in the best shops. It is called

Malden Salt, now untaxed, and, as the doctors tell us, unnecessary. Though not to me.

Writing in the Sand

IT IS ONLY St John's Gospel that credits Pilate with the authorship of the inscription on the Cross, 'Jesus of Nazareth the King of the Jews'. Artists could not get their brushes round this; so they painted INRI – Iesus Nazarenus Rex Iudaeorum.

And it is John only who records Pilate's obscure reply to the Jewish protest: 'What I have written, I have written.' This, and the Roman governor's other sayings, continue to lend him enormous interest. Something impenetrable to us was going on between him and the accused.

The only time we have Christ writing is with his finger in the sand. I always write my name in the sand-table in Dennington Church, on which the village children learnt their letters. Geoffrey Chaucer's family came from Dennington; so one would expect some literacy.

The church is fascinating, because very little has been turned out over the centuries, hence this sand-table. I listen with alarm when a priest, often a newcomer, casts his eye on our possessions. How the Dennington sand-table has survived spring-cleaning, heaven only knows. But there it is, eloquently suggesting the divine finger as well as countless little hands, now all dust.

The famous writer on the radio tells us of his delight when he closes his office door and picks up his fountain-pen. During a turnout, I found my Parker pen and my last dip-pen, and tenderly returned them to the beloved confusion that I call my stationery drawer. Each had written books.

The fountain-pen contained a withered lung, but was shiny and golden without. The dip-pen was encrusted with Quink. After ballpoints, the one felt fat and the other skinny between the fingers. I buy the ballpoints in sixes, and throw them away when they are no longer any use to me. Never have they attracted my love, although they too have written books.

I possess quite a number of new Relief- and J-nibs, but not a drop of ink. Did Virginia Woolf use Stephens' ink? Iris Murdoch used pencil – as did most of the soldiers on the Western Front, as they wrote their poems and forbidden diaries. Pencils are soft or hard and beautiful. A number of these, some very ancient, with rubbers in a tin crown on the top, sprout from a brass shell-case.

But what did Jesus write in the sand? If only one knew. It would change everything, I sense. It was after he had prevented a woman's being stoned. At Dennington, there is a smoother for obliterating what a finger has written. But Iesus Nazarenus Rex Iudaeorum in Hebrew, Greek, and Latin – not even the April weather would have blotted this out as the papyrus fluttered about Golgotha. What the strange governor had written he had certainly written, a gritty riposte to the mob.

Greeks wrote with a stylus – it is where style comes from. Every hand was different. I have never quite understood 'handwriting'; for what other kind of writing could there be? Computer-writing, some would say. How my heart went out to the famous writer with the fountain-pen. Was it Michael Morpurgo? Should I take my Parker to the ink-lung factory and try my hand with it, after all these rollerball years? Or fit a new nib into the murky holder, and feel it floating over the foolscap as it once did, soft and free?

The Passion

NEVER such an April. Perpetual sunshine, some of it hot; today's not so, although brilliant all the same. It lines the birds' wings and gilds the pear blossom. Yesterday, the merest feathering of rain on my face. The ancient farm track is Saharan with pale dust. And such pear blossom! The little valley orchard is on tiptoes, drawn up in its longing for light, or its need to see what is going on in Little Horkesley, to amazing limits. This will be fruit that cannot be picked, but must fall.

Preaching on Passion Sunday, I mention the Socratic nature of 'If it be thy will, let this cup pass from me.' This said by the one who only hours before had instituted the Cup of Life. Those who had drunk from it were a few yards away in the night air, worn out, while he, the giver, sweated blood at the thought of the prospect before him.

Right from the start, the Church has done its level best to walk closely with Christ because of this natural inability to do so in the darkening olive orchard. At this moment, the main characters in the awful drama were taking up their positions: the pain-blunted soldiers in the flogging room; the Jewish high priest in the Temple; the complex Pilate; the alarmed mother and women friends; the distinguished Joseph from Arimathaea.

There were elements of hurry, of swift dispatch, of getting the wretched business over. The Passover was about to begin, and dead bodies must be out of sight. They defiled the feast. We sang 'We may not know, we cannot tell, What pains he had to bear,' and the lovely spring day lit the Victorian glass. My dear friend Nell's funeral had taken place this week, and it was all death and life, life and death, wherever I looked. Blackness and brightness.

Once, the young teacher who was the Christ had asked a woman for a cup of water from, for him, a forbidden well. They had a lively exchange – she was used to men. He said he could give her a cup from which she would be able to drink life itself. What a gift, she thought. Never to have to walk all this way to the well every day!

It was Jacob's well, but the Samaritans had seized it long ago. It was, in fact, natural water in the desert, and nobody's well. Lost cups, similar to the one that he had shared with his friends at their Passover meal, would no doubt be lying in it, their clay splitting. Poetically, he had held out a similar cup to the bemused woman – 'Drink from this, and you will never thirst again.'

All these pre-Easter days he offers those who live by his teachings the terrible refreshment of his own blood. All around in the glorious East Anglian churches they are singing Bach's Passion music. A sea of cars islands the concert-goers. Light refreshments during the interval. We sing Isaac Watts's peerless 'When I survey the wondrous cross' – he had set Paul's words to the Galatians – and they leave me drained, as usual. Others too, no doubt.

Both Henry, the Vicar, and I brush against a crucifix whenever we climb the pulpit. It ceases to horrify us. We – all of us – are used to it: the naked tortured God, the defiled man. It is part of the fittings. Watts draws our attention to it: 'See from his head, his hands, his feet, Sorrow and love flow mingled down.'

MAY

Little Gidding Pilgrims

'IF YOU came this way,' wrote the poet famously, '. . . you would find the hedges White again, in May, with voluptuary sweetness.' And he was right. It is the feast of Matthias, the otherwise anonymous man chosen to mend the broken circle, and we are on pilgrimage to Little Gidding.

The verges wave with cow parsley, the clouds are mountainous, and red kites are acrobatic. It really is the most marvellous tramp. At Steeple Gidding, I watch the procession breast a grassy hill, a happy 'over the top', and I hear the litany being blown about as it descends to the redundant church. Young and old, familiar nameless faces, often beautiful, enter its cold space. Then the last lap to where Eliot found that 'prayer is more than an order of words'.

The Bishop of Peterborough lays flowers on Nicholas Ferrar's tombstone. The Ferrar brothers and George Herbert were Westminster schoolboys who could hardly have expected to end up here in Huntingdonshire.

Part of their education was to be crocodiled along the Thames path by Lancelot Andrewes, learning all the way. And, rather to my surprise, for one can become blasé about modern pilgrimage and its attempt to get into step with another age, I find myself also learning all the way.

I have, as a matter of fact, come this way a number of times without moving on from literature into faith. But today it is different. It must be the tumultuous weather, the realization that our route is the one that Nicholas rode on his horse when, at his old schoolfriend's careful instruction, he cancelled the ruin of Leighton Bromswold.

This was where our pilgrimage began. To somehow lift the meanness of Bemerton it had been decided to give Herbert the prebendal church of Leighton Bromswold.

It was wrecked, needless to say. Everything they gave him was in disorder, the priesthood most of all. He probably never saw Leighton Bromswold, but today we certainly saw him. I preached from the right-hand pulpit, looking down on the wide aisle. He had told Nicholas to think of Isaiah 35 when he got the builders to make it.

'And an highway shall be there, and a way, and it shall be called the Way of Holiness . . . it shall be for the wayfaring men . . . but the redeemed shall walk there.'

Herbert's pale benches bank this purposeful aisle, and his greenish glass casts a springtime light. We move from his handsome nave to his purposeful sanctuary for the eucharist. Shorts, big boots, dog-leads, packs. Now and then I find myself wondering 'what the dead had no speech for when living', as the lovely familiar words that Herbert 'set' in his verse are said yet again.

At Little Gidding, five miles away, another feat awaits, plus for myself a destination loaded with language. Such imagery. Such inescapable sentences and songs and memories and friendships. Herbert would have been delighted. 'Delight' was high in his vocabulary. Although young, he could not walk far, owing to the 'mole working away in his breast', that is, TB.

Francis Kilvert in Springtime

SOME WRITERS are as attached to the seasons as certain plants. Or so it seems to me. Charles Dickens to winter; Henry James to summer – 'Summer afternoon, summer afternoon; to me those have always been the two most beautiful words in the English language'; Barbara Pym to autumn, preferably in north Oxford, where tepid clergymen shuffle through fallen leaves to evensong; and Francis Kilvert to spring, although why this is, I cannot quite explain, as he is, in his Welsh-border way, a man for all seasons.

But spring becomes him. His life was brief and fresh, bright and dark by turn, and suddenly gone. I see him opening up like the chestnut blossom in our churchyard at this moment, then no more.

Now and then I read the congregation suitable bits from his lively Diary. Not this bit:

> May Day 1870. Mr Welby is rather given to light clerical slang and playfully alludes to his gown as his 'black' which he did not much approve of preaching in.
>
> He brought his own robes to church in a bundle and wore a cassock in which I should think he must have been uncommonly cold sitting in the chancel . . . His voice has a peculiar faculty for stirring up every echo in the church to make it indistinct and defeat itself.

Luncheon was equally unfortunate. Somebody had decanted cider in mistake for wine. Ah well. I used to stay near Clyro with an artist friend. Her house had been a manse attached to a

Nonconformist chapel in which the services still took place; so on the sabbath we sang along with the hymns on the other side of the wall. The Black Mountain loomed near by.

Young Kilvert walked every day of the year, and through all seasons. But his May Day walks were damp and luscious. He was tall and strong and sociable, and in his mid-thirties. And, like all the great diarists, a chronic recorder. Fragments of telling talk were tucked away in his head until he got back to his study.

May Day 1875. In the afternoon, I called at the Peckingell Farm and cottages. Farmer Austin told me that one day when he was expressing a wish for some rain, the maidservant, who objected to rain because the men came in with muddy boots . . . said to him, 'Master, why do you want so much rain? You be always crying out for rain.' 'Maid,' said the old farmer, severely, 'I do want rain on this here farm every night. Yes, I do want rain on this here farm every night.'

Duncan has been saying much the same thing to me, nearly a century-and-a-half later. It has been June in April, and the valley bakes. It was on a similar blazing May morning when John Couzens, a farmworker, told the young curate how fond he was of dry bread – as dry and hard as he could get it. 'When I was out mowing, I used to throw my wallet and victuals on the swath and let the sun bless it from bait to bait. I wanted it all crust.'

The Kilvert Society, of which I am president, will be tramping in Francis's footsteps this May, but I cannot be with them. It is a tidy step from the Stour to the Wye.

'As I came down from the hill into the valley, a great wave of emotion and happiness stirred and rose up within me. I know not why . . .'

Robert Louis Stevenson in Samoa

I WEED my way to the honeysuckle that the German prisoners of war planted for Christine, the kind lady who spoke their language and made them cakes. The honeysuckle's scent amazes me as I free the labyrinthine plant from nettles.

Down in the village, they are creating the Flower Festival. Forget Chelsea; pity neighbouring parishes. Wormingford's annual extravaganza is known to be unequalled. The theme this year is local history – Sutton Hoo, and all that. Tea will be served on table tombs. Arrangers will do the most unlikely things.

Strolling around, I will be forced to see my neighbours with new eyes. However did such notions of the past get into their heads? Looming over all is the Quota. We don't do these wonderful things just for fun, they are saying.

Back at Bottengoms Farm, I discover one of those calf-bound late-Victorian books that are kept but never read. It is *Prayers Written at Vailima*, by Robert Louis Stevenson (Chatto and Windus, 1894). Their beauty lies in their confidence, and also, of course, in their having been written down by a master of English.

After briefly describing their origin, I read three of them at the Flower Festival service, and their richness makes me realize what a 'thinning' of faith has occurred since Stevenson summoned his household to prayer, and now.

He had sailed to Samoa to prolong his life, taking with him

his wife, stepson, and widowed mother, and on a ship straight out of Treasure Island. On Samoa, he built a huge, flimsy, leafy mansion, which immediately filled with charming retainers. It was with a native war-trumpet that all were called to these prayers.

The Samoans are very fierce and very religious, and quite enchanted by Tusitala – the storyteller – plus all the food. They wear a single garment and flowers and leaves, and powder their hair with lime. Tusitala presides at the top of a long room, and hears 'the long rambling Samoan hymn rolling up to him', and they hear his lovely prayers rolling down to them.

No room for them here. But here is a snatch of 'Evening'. Imagine the author of *Catriona* (and *The Strange Case of Dr Jekyll and Mr Hyde*) in his leaf-palace, his lungs almost gone, saying in his Edinburgh voice:

> Lord, receive our supplications for this house, family, and country. Protect the innocent, restrain the greedy and the treacherous, lead us out of our tribulation into a quiet land.
>
> Look down upon ourselves and upon our absent dear ones ... Give us health, food, bright weather, and light hearts ... Let us lie down without fear, and awake and arise with exultation. For his sake, in whose words, we now conclude.

Very soon, hearing of the death of a friend, he wrote:

> Strange that you should be beginning a new life, when I, who am a little your junior, am thinking of the end of mine. But I have had hard lines; I have been so long waiting for death; I have unwrapped my thoughts from about life so long, that

I have not a filament left to hold by . . . Literally, no man has more wholly outlived life than I. And still it's good fun.

He was 44 when the Samoans carried their Tusitala to the hilltop.

That Equal Music

ROUGH WINDS have been shaking the darling buds of May with a vengeance. They have been roaring through the oaks and hooting up the valley. Swallows are saying, 'Well, this is a good welcome!' and dream of the soft oceanic currents that carried them to Bottengoms. The sun, when it gets a chance to shine through the tumult, is hot.

I have been doing the great spring weed, advancing through the nettles with Roger's scythe, slaying all before me, but here and there, like some just conqueror, permitting a patch of this or that to survive. Rogation is past. We have done with our asking.

The bluebell party at Tiger Hill has broken up, and we are scattered for another year, these annual friends whose names come and go like lines from an infrequently sung hymn. But we saw the cold stream, may have heard the nightingale, and definitely warmed to each other.

Believing it appropriate, I brought a bottle of home-made wine, one mouthful of which flew to my head. When the others had a sip, they said, 'Oh, gosh,' and things like that. The woodland floor swayed a bit.

At the country funeral, I recited John Donne's incomparable 'Bring us, O Lord God, at our last awakening into the house and gate of heaven, to enter into that gate and dwell in that house, where there shall be no darkness nor dazzling, but one equal light . . .'

In a city, a funeral takes place almost without a soul noticing. A hearse passes. In a village, a funeral takes place with everybody noticing. A familiar figure passes. A funeral is often the most cliché-ridden of our rites of passage. How to restore its gravitas? How to bring back Donne's 'one equal music, possession, eternity'? Our robes fly about in the graveyard wind. Henry, the Vicar, talks of the dead as being beyond our experience.

I open the Mary Newcomb exhibition in Norwich. She is one of those artists who extends or astounds our experience, filling in the gaps of our observation with what we did not think worthy of our attention. Not least the amount of idleness, of doing nothing, which takes up much of our time in the countryside.

Badly dressed women going – where? A bike and its attendant. Poorly maintained sheds, cafés, gardens. Sly dogs. Dragonflies in their glory. And a great stillness.

The subjects are those of a naïve painter such as the Cornish Albert Wallis, yet Mary Newcomb is (was, for she has recently gone to where there is that equal music and light) a scientist, and her Suffolk is intellectually informed – but by what? This is the excitement of her work.

We had only just begun to know each other when she was struck dumb by a stroke. It was tantalizing. To have so much to say, and then just to smile. But these roomfuls of pictures in Norwich – what a marvellous confession of what she saw in life!

The chilly days have persuaded the white cat to return to semi-hibernation. She wakes to eat. Otherwise she is in a deep sleep on a velvet stool. 'Is your cat OK?' asks a little boy. I'll say.

The flower festival looms, and John is knocking in signs along the approach roads to the church. Women look lustingly at my alliums. The great barn is being cleared for Phyllida's mighty bargains. Soon the flower arrangers will be dining on a table-tomb.

Getting Lost

THE WORLD changed for the worse when it began to talk of time instead of distance. When it said 'Twenty-four hours' to Sydney instead of 'Thousands of miles'. Six hours to Edinburgh. The word 'diary' descends from the Latin diarium. This became 'journal', a day's account; and 'journey', a day's travel.

When my mother sailed to Sydney in the 1950s, it took her six weeks to cross the earth. Now, it has taken 'a handful of dust' to dethrone travel time and to reinstate travel distance. People who have forgotten miles are astounded when they have to deal with them – that everywhere is a long way.

Previous to the object lesson thrown up in Iceland, the difficulties of getting from Italy to England were, for most of today's travellers, puzzling. We have all sat next to some time-bore on a plane as he whines about our being an hour late. Now, in the planeless world in which I am writing, lateness has become irrelevant, and roads humbling. To get anywhere except by air, we learn, is exhausting and very expensive. And yet something is gained – travel as distance.

I thought of J. H. Newman, aged 32, stranded in Sicily, and more upset than he thought he would be by parting from his friends the Froudes, who were going on, as they say. It was all arranged, this break. Newman became delirious, to weep and yet to assure his servant, 'I shall not die, for I have not sinned against the light.' It was late May 1833, and he kept saying that he had work to do in England.

But Oxford from Castro Giovanni, which we have been estimating as a couple of hours, was a huge journey. Newman walked, and got lifts to Palermo, where he had to wait for three weeks before an orange-boat could take him to Marseilles. It is a famous travel tale. While the orange-boat was becalmed for a week in the Straits of Bonifacio, 'I wrote the lines "Lead, kindly Light", which have since become well known. I was writing verses the whole time of my passage.'

He was, of course, making a dual journey: one to his mother's house in London, one to Rome. He reached the former in early July. The next Sunday, 14 July, he was in Oxford to hear John Keble's electrifying sermon.

'Lead, kindly Light' caused as much questioning as devotion when it reached the hymn books. Especially the line, 'And with the morn those Angel faces smile.' Were they poor Mrs Tait's five children who had all died in the spring of 1856? She was the wife of the Dean of Carlisle, and the tragedy had swept the Church of England.

Newman refused to explain. He said: 'Anyhow, there must be a statute of limitation for writers of verse, or it would be quite tyranny if in an art, which is the expression, not of truth, but of imagination and sentiment, one were obliged to be ready for examination on the transient states of mind which came upon one when homesick or seasick . . .' William Barry said of 'Lead, kindly Light': 'This most tender of pilgrim songs may be termed the March of the Tractarian Movement. It is pure melody, austere yet hopeful.'

What were the other poems Newman wrote on the sluggish

orange-boat? What did the Sicilian sailors make of him, this upset young Englishman?

Matings – Boys, Girls and Birds

A JOHN CONSTABLE morning. Cumulus clouds heap up on each other, then break to allow the blue to appear in a vast restlessness. He insisted that the sky was the keynote to the land, colourfully speaking.

I see him striding over the hill towards his uncle's farm in his white clothes, turning the women's eyes. Like the skies, his personality was one that chopped and changed, thrilled and meditated, to the rolling displays of the weather.

When young in the Stour Valley, he would carry a little palm-fitting sketchbook in which he would pencil the earth and the heavens. When no longer young, he would paint the racing clouds over Hampstead Heath on oiled paper, having to invent wild brush-strokes to keep up with them. Below Hampstead, London miasma denied the existence of the aerial mountains and cerulean apertures to the country of the hymn book.

Preparing something for Sunday, I let Matthias, Dunstan, Alcuin, and Helena drift across my retina. Who will be the lucky one to get a mention? Dear great saints, bright unclouded creatures, shine on.

Nippy final frosts. As I drive with John from the Norfolk coast, the Saturday afternoon roads are all scrubbed up by heavy rain. We journey across country, knowledgeably below drenched trees, hardly meeting another car. Where is every-body? At the football.

Whitebait and Guinness in the Lavenham pub. Young lovers. Trumpets and other instruments dangling from the beams to remind us that Lavenham's Salvationists still play on the Market Square. And two Salvationists from Northumbria at our matins the following morning, singing well. Plus a party to hear the bans. New faces. How could we know of an impediment to their marriage or anything about them? Oh, the excitement of a Jane Eyre figure bursting in!

A century ago, the Church of England became disturbed by the number of village lovers marrying far from their home parish, fed up with nosiness, and Dean Hole of Rochester applauded the bicycle as a liberator of the rural male from local restrictions.

Banns is a medieval word for proclamation. It was sometimes used for the prologue of a play. The wedding could raise the curtain on a comedy or a tragedy, although usually something quite ordinary, as Philip Larkin saw on the station platform one Whitsun long ago.

My wood is restless with mating birds. Their voices are raised over belated bluebells, and indignantly, should I garden late in the evening. I have cast a bit of wire netting over the potato mounds, just in case the badgers heave into them, hungry for worms.

May is an enticing time, and I can hardly bear to be inside. But it is cold. No sitting about. Work, work, and no shedding a clout – i.e. a jersey. David arrives hot-foot from a meeting of the Cambridge Prayer Book Society and a lecture by Angela Tilby at St John's College. She is one of those people who make things believable. It is something they do without knowing it – this beautiful passing on of what they understand.

He has brought rhubarb from his London allotment, which

you might think was coals to Newcastle. But mine needs a week or two more. It, too, is badger guarded. The badgers huff and puff in their setts at twilight.

Our Flower Festival

THE TEMPERATURE has dropped from 80°-something to 40°-something, and all in a day. The ancient house is cool and daring me to switch on the heating – or even put a match to the fire. Gloire de Dijon roses burst against its walls.

On Sunday, the farmer searching for Isaiah in the lectern Bible before Pentecostal evensong says: 'Pray for rain.' No fear. Oh, the sun, the sun! He reads about God's omniscience. 'Behold, the nations are as a drop of a bucket, and are counted as the small dust of the balance: behold he taketh up the isles as a very little thing . . .' There are times when I could listen to Isaiah by the hour. Night birds sing in the late garden.

Later in the week – when it gets chilly – I watch the Queen turning pages with her gloves on, and promising dire changes in a low voice. The Lord Chancellor, more gorgeous than anyone can remember, has delivered this little booklet to her. 'Behold, I will make thee a new sharp threshing instrument having teeth', says Isaiah, and every new government.

This one is full of boys and girls, very youthful and hopeful, and at this moment at odds with what it is hearing. The Queen asks the Almighty to bless it, then slowly departs to trumpet-music. And I switch off to weed. I have a similar guilt at watching daytime television to that of the Victorians about reading novels in the morning.

Chelsea and our village Flower Show are in preparation at

this hour. Neither is giving a thought to the other. Mountains of flowers bend to the arrangers' wish. Canvas creaks in the heat; aisles that so recently echoed to Veni, Creator Spiritus clank with watering cans. The diocesan Moloch demands his due.

At neighbouring Long Melford, a debt is paid with a single rose. We at Wormingford depend on countless flowers to pay the Quota. The poet John Clare used to pay the rent with apples when the pennies ran out. This at Michaelmas. 'Comfort ye, comfort ye, my people,' says Isaiah's God, but do not forget that 'The grass withereth, the flower fadeth because the spirit of the Lord bloweth upon it.'

Pentecost is a gale, a tempest of language. Isaiah liked to join in birdsong. 'Like a crane or a swallow, so did I chatter.' There is a marvellous sequential birdsong in my huge ash at about seven o'clock every evening, run upon run. Who sings it? Some brother to the nightingale? I must ask Pam.

In Sydney, I visited a natural-history museum where there was a room full of stuffed birds. When you pressed a button, they sang. It was terrible. Isaiah said that when he was depressed he mourned like a dove and that his eyes failed from looking on the bright side. One knows the feeling.

The farmers who toiled here century after century would have been too dog-tired at the end of the day to enjoy a bit of depression. They would have nodded off on the porch-seat in the failing light, the collie's head warm on their knee. The may-trees would be blinding-white in the meadow. Just as they are today. And the sexy May scent would be everywhere, and the plum blossom would have set.

Taking One's Time

TAKING matins the other day, I found myself rather hoping that there would not be too much cheerfulness around the throne. More a paced Herbertian happiness. Slowing down worship in order that one can dream and think is a hard task. Making spaces. Now and then, although usually long ago, someone caught up in eternity while still alive due to being in church, will stop the service galloping along.

At Hoo, in Suffolk, there was a farmworker lesson-reader who, lost in sacred language and indifferent to the clock, would look up from the lectern and say: 'That was very fine. I'll read that again.' And did, to our joy.

They say that Thomas Hardy's services in Stinsford (Mellstock) church would have been a drag to us. The fiddles and rich labouring voices at the west end, the sparks flying from iron-tipped Sunday boots, the packed singing pews, the holy sabbath leisure.

Would he have become our greatest rural novelist if he had been hurried along at evensong and not allowed time to look at girls, or at a wall monument to a boy named Angel? Or especially at the marble skull on the monument to Audeley and Margaret Grey? Edward Springrove stood under it as he watched Manston's and Cytherea's wedding in *Desperate Remedies*.

Now we rush. Should the leaves of the hymn book stick together, and time pass infinitesimally before I announce 'Breathe on me, breath of God', there is the faintest of faint concern for the worship speedometer.

When I first came to Wormingford, there was an ancient vicar, holy enough in his own way, who would call out 'Last verse' immediately after we had sung the first. I have been in country churches where the dreamlike nature of a service is so heaven-preparing that I could not bear them to stop.

Let it not be said that I impose this advanced Anglicanism on my dear Sunday friends, however, although once a dreamer, always a dreamer, and there's no cure for that.

The white cat sleeps and dreams 23 hours a day; sometimes on me, sometimes under a rose. And five horses stand on the horizon, their tails spun into gold by the May sun. Are they sleeping or gossiping? And a cuckoo cries on and on. And nobody, unlike in *The Archers*, does a stroke of work on the land, which produces all that we need in perfect rows, without toil.

I plant out my runner beans, my seeds of all sorts. People call. Cold callers on the telephone impudently enquire about my money. Or my kitchen. Like the character in the poem, I read much of the night and go south in the morning. South, that is, to where I planted my 'Sir Cedric Morris' rose to see if it is flourishing. As a youth, I watched it more than flourish in his garden, go off on its own spitefully prickly way, a cascade of lovely, cruel blooms over his sheds. It is doing fine.

Orange boards along the road divert the rushing cars to our Flower Festival, the theme of which is the Benedicite. It is on 30 May, if you can make it. 'O ye holy and humble Men of heart, bless ye the Lord: praise him, and magnify him for ever.' And take your time about it. It will help you to live longer. And now to breakfast, for it is past eight o'clock.

JUNE

Wide, Wide as the Ocean

SEA SUNDAY. The news that Mike the churchwarden and his boat were stranded on a sand bank at Harwich had not quite sunk in as I announced the processional. But I could say 'Eternal Father, strong to save' without irony.

The multi-tasked organist and bellringers brought the peal to a close, the clock struck 11, the sun shone bright, and we were away. William Whiting's sonorous hymn, pleading and fearful, filled the church.

He was a small, bespectacled master of the Winchester choristers, who had nothing to do with the sea, yet he was able to convey its terror. The French Navy adores his hymn:

Vois nos pleurs, entends nos sanglots,
Pour ceux en péril sur les flots

rose from their men-of-war. He was 35 when he wrote it. Why? Because so many of his pupils would be sailing away to run the Empire?

Such oceans, such wrecks, such spaces without communication. We cannot imagine it. All that we can see, if we can see anything at all, is white drill, the captain's table, brave pennants, and deck quoits. We have other fears. The psalm is 65. 'Who stilleth the raging of the sea: and the noise of the waves, and the madness of the people', and then, 'The river of God is full of water.'

I think of Conrad's fastidious voyagers, young men with a past, or with a future, who give nothing away in the crowded ports and cabins; and Robert Louis Stevenson and his family sailing to Samoa in order to lengthen his existence. The party included his Edinburgh mother, widow of the lighthouse-builder.

No other writer can beat Stevenson at describing the sound of the sea, the tumultuous surface, the horrifying groans of its deeps, and the ecstatic commotion of the birds – although William Golding can run him close. I met him once: a whiskery old sea-captain of a novelist, with clear blue eyes and a patient wife. It was she who proposed the story that became *Lord of the Flies*, a desert-island turn-around tale in which, and contrary to Ballantyne's *The Coral Island*, stranded British boys have no difficulty in becoming 'savages'.

But back to church. There is leg of lamb in the slow oven, and mint sauce in the larder. And their ravishing odour should not be drifting into the chancel. But the East Coast smells too – a sharp intake of pure cold and a whiff of fish.

I think of the Lord by Galilee, and his netting four fishermen disciples all on a single day. And of this inland lake's capricious storms, and nobody able to swim, as this had been the policy of seafarers since sailing began. For to swim when the ship went down meant a dreadful protraction of drowning. Nelson could not swim.

Air travel has tended to obliterate the beauties and terrors of sea travel, and all in a few decades. Although 'travel' is not the right word for modern flight. To reach India from Stansted in a day is not travel, although what it is is hard to describe. The network of shipping routes which skeined the oceans for so long are no longer travelled as we rush along the flight paths of the sky. As far as I know, there is no 'Eternal Father, strong to save' for these journeys.

Mother never set off for Felixstowe without asking God for what she called 'journeying mercies', and I doubt if there is not much silent prayer at take-offs and landings. Or on the motorway.

Stay-at-homes, too, have their fears. The poet John Clare found the sun to be in the wrong place when he left his village. All movement brings disorientation.

A Sunday Walk with Henry James

NEAR-BLUDGEONED to death by didactic Starkey history, I find my copy of Owen Chadwick's *Reformation* to get my head right before falling asleep.

I read: 'Linacre, the physician of King Henry VIII, had been rector of four parishes, a canon of three cathedrals, and precentor of York Minster before he was ordained priest. He was receiving payment for his medical services by this variety of rectories and prebends.'

Cowed as I am at this moment, the listener-viewer in the pew (on the sofa) will be in dire need of some quieter intelligence in order to get his head straight. Thus Owen Chadwick in his small masterpiece *The Reformation*. It provides not so much the required pinch of salt for much telly-history as a brief spread of the full canvas, the invention of printing and all.

For me, it was really the invention of the printed book which did it, not those often manic efforts of an ill king to establish his line. His subjects were coming to that point when they would adore literature more than anything else in the world. And so, when Henry commanded that an English Bible must be placed in every church in the land, he would all unknowingly lay the foundations of that Englishness which would express his people's soul.

Against this mighty achievement, all else is little more than dashed male vanity, bad gynaecology, early gifts gone to rot, and his having one foot in the old discredited magic and the other in the new science. And when he fathered poor Anne's disinherited daughter, he had no way of knowing that she would be the monarch he could not be. What the viewer needs is Owen Chadwick's still, small voice. Have you noticed how David Starkey talks like a Tudor? It would not surprise me if he finds himself in the Tower one of these schedules.

To calmer matters. Henry James, no less. These days, our country walks come peppered with hard facts. See that nice patch of bird's-foot-trefoil; look – there's a blackcap; let us visit the church with its famous long-and-short work. And now let us accompany Henry James, who doesn't walk very far or see very much. Or, to be fair, see what we see.

It is after luncheon in 1877, and there is grass in the middle of the lane, and never a car in sight. And he has no knowledge of wetlands, or Perp. and Dec., or botany, or segmented-headed windows in the Hall. All the same, as this walk was taken so long ago, he tell us things, being an American, about England which we have forgotten or will no longer be able to see.

This is why it is so delightful to walk in Warwickshire with him. The social classes are distinct. Labourers' children giving him a bob. Almshouse folk reminding him of Trollope. Well-bred beauties on the tennis court, who are the perfect stock for his heroes and heroines, the flushed whiteness of the girls, the white goldenness of the boys – something you would never find in New York. Soon they will wed and provide patriots for the Western Front.

It usually rains when Henry James walks in Warwickshire. On Sunday afternoons, he accompanies his hosts to evensong, and sits with them in a box pew. But no description of the service. His heaven is a gentleman's park, and he is scathing about an earl who prefers London's gaming clubs to his country seat. Henry walks to it. It hides behind a wall of ivy. In the park, he muses on cathedrals and castles, and is barely informative, but entrancing.

'When are We Going to Framlingham Castle?'

THE SUMMER beats down. Birds call in the wood. The clickety-clack of Duncan's old haymaker ceases, like all human endeavours in Ecclesiastes, and is followed by an interesting silence. All the old roses are in full sway. William Lobb, John Clare, and Cardinal Richelieu cense the garden. I read novels in the sun. Fiscal illiteracy protects me from the News.

My Australian nephew, William, is brought to see his uncle. He is ten and solemn. What would he most like to see in England? A castle. Colchester, Hedingham, Framlingham?

Framlingham. A good choice, little boy. The curtain walls will have gathered the heat and the tourists and, long ago, let out the dukes. This noble castle housed princes, and did service for a workhouse in its day, and is now what is called heritage.

But most things are heritage, one way and another. I give William a beautiful box of Victorian dominoes made of ivory. He opens it warily. His face is turned to Framlingham. His mother says: 'Say thank you.' Thank you. 'How far is it to Framlingham?'

Try as I might, the Veterans' Day service turns into a second 11 November. I gather in the Legions' standards and place them in the sanctuary. I preach on *The Years*, and a bugle sounds. Time, like an ever-rolling stream, bears all its sons away, though not yet, says Harold, pushing 92.

We all have to go to the Beehive pub first. Cars bake in the lane, and French marigolds on graves. And men who landed on the beaches or fought at Kohima drink bitter. 'To think', I had told them, 'that for most of the time we went to bed with the moon and got up with the sun, and then a great gold clock was fixed to the tower, and there were 60 minutes to the hour even when you were in the timeless fields.'

The Legionnaires had smartly collected their banners and marched away. To the Beehive, where Time is no longer called as in their youth.

The bar is cool and shady, like my old dairy, now the larder, which is richly scented with bowls of strawberries and cherries, Whiskas, and ancient bricks. 'There, William,' says his mother, 'what do you think of that? Uncle's pantry.'

'When are we going to Framlingham Castle?' Tomorrow. When one is ten, one is always going somewhere tomorrow.

Young Alban died this week. A Turin manuscript says that it

was in the year 209, during the Diocletianic attempt to destroy Christianity. Alban was a Romano-British soldier who followed Christ. He was stationed at Verulamium. He may have saved a priest's life by exchanging his uniform for his vestments. He was caught anyway, and beheaded on Holmhurst Hill, now the site of the Abbey.

We were once in the diocese of St Albans; so the soldier-saint stands attentively on our reredos, a memorial to the Revd Mr Tufnell, squire plus parson, who ruled Wormingford for half a century. Why aren't more boys named Alban? Once a year, in the summertime, our usually unrecognized soldier stares down at us through a mass of flowers. It would have been a hot day on Holmhurst Hill when they killed him. Untrustworthy historians spoke of strange happenings in the skies. I imagine it was the usual English June morning, things warming up, the hours promising after an execution.

Returning to the Home Ground

'SUMMER RAIN,' I observe to my neighbour. Had I done so to Grandmother, she would have said, 'Don't wish your life away,' for summer is still three weeks hence. How she valued time! The rain is soft and scented. Penetrating, too. It caresses the roses and laburnums without a sound. And it falls on the just and the unjust, of course.

The occupants of the nest box on the russet apple-tree put their beaks out now and then, eyeing the scene. The white horses steam. People in sodden clothes call and say, 'Summer rain!'

We have lunch at the Cock, Polstead, where a reporter from *The Times* wrote up the horrible murder of Maria Marten in the red barn for posterity. It rings few bells nowadays. And the cherry orchards, Polstead's other claim to fame, have long gone the same way as Chekhov's. George Herbert said: 'Nothing lasts except the Church.'

As we cannot get any wetter, David props up the Duchesse de Montenbello, and I stick the runner beans. We know our place. The flag on the tower is a sopping dishcloth. Its ropes are fraying and, says John, it looks like a trip to Brightlingsea to fetch new ones.

The dead lie deep down beyond rainfall, beyond seasons, or they have risen above it all, the perfumed earth, the weather, and all that. These villagers who would be clumping in to supper. There is a full moon a mite misshapen and bleary with rain, and there is Corpus Christi, and there is Thomas Ken with his morning and night songs to be sung at the window.

Politically speaking, the future is weird. Last week, it was 'O brave new world that has such people in't!', but this week it is 'Watch out!' Today, it is a flying return to Debach and Charsfield, the countryside in which I lived for many years and wrote poems and stories and *Akenfield*.

It is modest mid-Suffolk. The villages lie in hollows or on slight rises. My glorious elms have gone, and the old house stands rather naked by the Roman road. The Victorian church has turned into a house. I took its last evensong.

But the soft brick tower of Charsfield Church continues to warm to the passer-by, and the interior to the prayerful heart. Old friends lie around in the June grass. The school buzzes. Blossom sets into fruit on the trees. The shop has vanished. All my bike-rides sprint around. Signposts point to a younger self.

The vicarage no longer does its original duty – as do not so many places. But the common prosperity, now to be challenged in case we do a Greece or Ireland, has smartened up the parish. I greet and smile, wave, consider. 'You look well!'

And so on to show Antony Framlingham and Hoo. And wonderful Dennington, where we write with our fingers in the sand-tray where boys and girls learnt their letters, smoothing our names out with the smoother before we leave. Tottering, lovely, fretted screens, every kind of pew from carved bench to box and beyond. The freezing cold of the eight-o'clock.

This is where Geoffrey Chaucer's family, earthy folk from the surrounding fields, worshipped. They moved into the royal family via the wine trade. But I remember Daniel doing duty for the Rector, and myself 'putting the things out' for him.

The Authors of True Happiness

NO RAIN, but heavy dews. They raise an early sparkle. You might argue the great spring drought. Countless roses hang their soggy heads, and a drenched cat flies in from where she has spent an adventurous night, crying, 'Food, food, for pity's sake.' I water-in some marrow plants, and stick a few beans. The wind is icy, and the sun baking. The immense aspens make Delius sounds above my head, and drop tassels on the grass.

Back at the ranch, my study is a minute version of Hampton Court after Habakkuk, say, has been translated; for I have just finished the lecture on the Authorized Version which I must give in Norwich Cathedral next week. Is it long enough? Too short? Shall I wear an academic robe and bands and look like

Lancelot Andrewes; or wear my new blazer, and look smart-casual?

When Parson Woodforde was commanded to preach in the Cathedral by his bishop, he was amazed. The cheek of it! As if he hadn't enough to do in his parish, what with reading the office and dining with the neighbours.

Will I see the peregrines nesting on the spire? What a good year it is for birds.

Having put the study to rights and listened to a friend on the telephone assuring me that the end is nigh – the drought – I take a Barbara Pym into the garden. It is the novel about gentlewomen in London flats just after the war: youngish friends who run up curtains, worship in semi-bombed churches, arrange their few pieces of good furniture from the country vicarage, and wait for the boys to come home.

They dine on whale meat, Spam, and Ovaltine, and work in Learned Society offices. The Pym style is never as innocent as it looks. There are references to the *Church Times*, and to love.

Now and then, I turn a page and wonder if my lecture's references to King James may not be suitable for a cathedral. He had his faults, God only knows, but he was divine. I see him watching *The Tempest* at Whitehall, and thinking, erroneously, of course: 'Prospero – that's me!'

The Hampton Court translators laid on their dedication to James with a trowel, as people used to say. They said he was, under God, 'the immediate Author of their true happiness', and that he was 'as of the sun in his strength after the setting of that bright Occidental Star Queen Elizabeth', and much else.

My childhood Bible contained a great many unauthorized pages, such as delightful maps of the Holy Land, lists of its plants, pronunciations of its names, and, of course, this gorgeous flattery. I suppose that now and then the sermon would have entered my head, but I cannot remember it.

Mother was a devout Bible-reader, and could open it at Nehemiah or Peter 2 at once. Those were the days. Often, a reading here is so beautiful that I want it to go on for pages, and regret the sudden chord for the Te Deum, the need to stand, the brusque dismissal of the lonely voice.

In my lecture, I shall quote the old farm worker who, at the lectern, would pause and say: 'That was very fine – I'll read that again.' And did.

Our People

HAPPENING to be in their direction, we call on the ancestors, I and the Australian nephews. There they lie, below the sodden cow-parsley; for it has rained most of the night. The Suffolk churchyard begins with the bright slabs of the newly cremated, and concludes with the correct wilds of the set-aside.

A month ago, it would have looked enchanting, Queen Anne's lace and tottering marble, but now, owing to the blessed rain, it is a kind of stringy flower-porridge, which we rake aside with our hands in order to read the inscriptions.

Here is Uncle Frederick, who coughed his way back home from the Western Front. Gassed. Twenty-nine. Here is Great-uncle Henry Bean, very old. Here is Agnes, his wife, even older, who gave us bread and butter, not cake, and whose house smelled of 'keepers' – apples on shelves.

Here are the faint humps of boys and girls who, unlike the

day-old baby in Long Melford Church, are not recorded in stone. We trample over them, pollen sticking to our jeans. Human dust, botanical dust. 'Dust on an old man's sleeve.' But what a rain! I think of my runner-beans soaring up the cane wigwams, and of perpetual spinach breaking the surface, of the stream swooshing and the white cat not pleased.

Inside the church there is the fractured Saxon (possibly) font, and the Victorian font in which Mr Harper baptized me. And in the frame his photo, in profile. How alive he looks. And a long way off there is the famous brass of Sir Robert de Bures and his daughter Dame Alyse, cosy under rugs. I rubbed them on to kitchen paper with heelball from Mrs Diaper, who mended our boots. Sir Robert died in 1302. He lived when Marco Polo returned to Venice after staying with Kublai Khan, when paper money was invented, and when the popes were at their zenith.

I forget to tell my nephew Michael about the paper money. He is the chief investment manager of an Australian bank, and here he is, wet to the knees to study his forebears.

All around us, drowned in rainy plants, lie shepherds and ploughmen, parsons and gypsies, lovers and gossips, listening to showers and birds, sheep and history. I used to like to imagine that I could hear the click-clack of looms when I was a teenage historian; for this was deep wool-country. They said that I was fanciful – their very word. It was not a compliment.

I must now write a foreword to a book about Virginia Woolf's holiday wanderings – sometimes in a Bloomsbury group, now and then on her own. And always rather uncomfortable. Too much luggage, too big bicycles, too studied an indifference to what most of us saw, though intensely readable, all the same.

She studied hard not to see a church of the Church of England. But she never missed seeing into the people she met. They were never surfaces to her. And, naturally, it rained. Those damply dragging long tweed skirts, those chilly bedrooms, those orders and complaints of the upper-middle-class away from home, those demanding diaries on the bedside table.

They would take you back if it wasn't so long ago, further in some ways than Sir Robert de Bures. But travel it was. Looking it was. Commotion and stillness it was. Life and death it was. Just getting about in these islands.

The End of a Syllabus

AND SO it has come to pass. St Andrew's Church of England Primary School, Wormingford, has ceased to be. For a year or so, it bragged about being the smallest school in the county – 13 pupils – which would have made the education committee look at its books. But I looked at the work on its walls and marvelled at its beauty, the art and natural history, the painfully brilliant lettering of its poetry, the repetitive recreation of our village myth, George and the Dragon.

On such evidence, I could believe that our school could go on for ever. But 13 boys and girls . . . And who of us has seen them, skyed as they are in the bedrooms, eyes fixed on screens, small hands on mice? You might catch a glimpse of them at the Nine Lessons and Carols.

The attendance was about 35 when I was a school governor, and when I occasionally walked over the footpaths to tell stories, or take assemblies. The teachers lived many miles away and, through no fault of their own, failed to be 'local'. Churchwise, they could not have been called parishioners.

As in countless villages, there is an unreachable element, certainly to someone of my generation. Nor should I attempt to reach it; for it is not for me. For one who is a historian and poet, however, our soon-to-be-emptied classrooms will stay full of voices.

The young men on the war memorial will continue to sing in them. The strictly required songs on the Syllabus will for ever beat against the church windows; for the Syllabus was, of course, a holy law. It would, for generations, have hung on a tack in the chalks cupboard, swinging whenever the door opened, saying: 'Thou shalt not teach anything other than me.'

The 1870 Education Act astounded the farmers. Since when did boys and girls not pick up stones on their fields to mend the lanes, scare rooks, or work? Not to labour until they were 12 years old! There was rural war.

There were also many rural schools, with some made-up 'syllabus' by the rector, or often by his wife, which preceded Whitehall, such as that which John Clare attended in Glinton vestry for a penny a week. And he taught himself arithmetic on the dusty walls of the threshing-barn. Paper was the great country poet's need, and paper was stingily handed out for decades in village schools such as ours. First, slates, then, dazzlingly, an exercise book and ink. To blot your copybook was your first crime.

Our school is lasting Victorian Gothic. Flints from our fields glitter in both sun and rain. Sleeping policemen make sure that it is approached at one mile an hour, thus reverently. All the years I have known it, the religious element has been cautious and courteous, and getting the children over the road and into the church a near impossibility.

The old sense of belonging is chiefly expressed in weddings and funerals. Or by the new families in our manors – we have about five. The school has simply died out, has done what first the Syllabus demanded it to do, then what governors such as I required it to do. But its institutional purpose just faded, as bigger schools got, well, bigger. And these ten minutes away in the car.

When I commiserated with a neighbour about our loss, she wondered where we could hold our flower-show refreshments. I wondered about nearly a century-and-a-half's boys and girls.

Do Quakers Sing?

THE DROUGHT has vanished, and the wheat on the dipping field doesn't look half bad. It has taken its normal midsummer blue-green colour, and has what scripture calls 'fatness'. Immense clouds sail over it, plus a snowy glider or two. Sudden showers, hot sunshine, movement – too much of the latter, in our parish of Mount Bures, where badgers threaten the 'motte' of a castle with their own building plans. But the countryside, after being static and swamped, is drying out and on the go.

Friends in the double sense have been showing me the new extension to the Meeting House at Bury St Edmunds. That captured quietness! Quakerism is a world apart, and also a world within a world, making its presence felt.

The architect of the restoration was required to create 'an outward expression of our Quaker values to peace, truth, integrity, simplicity, equality, community, and stewardship of the earth and its resources'. How does one line up all this on paper? How is quietness 'housed'? In many ways, of course, but here in a famously principled way.

I step inside, and am met with Georgian separateness and with 21st-century inclusion. The joining rooms are tall and still, pale and severe. The old seating is rectangular, the new circular. The Suffolk light pours in. Outside, there is a fine garden and, say the Friends who are my friends, 'a chip shop and a sex shop'.

And a cathedral. And an altar where they drew up Magna Carta. And a wall where I propped my bike when I was a teenager. And these wandering skies, which, in his mysterious way, God makes big with mercy so as to break with blessings on our heads.

'Do Quakers sing at Meeting?'

'Yes, if the spirit says so.'

'Read a poem?'

'Read a poem.'

I often read about James Parnell, the Quaker boy they murdered in Colchester. He is one of my heroes. 'Ye fearful saints, fresh courage take,' is what I used to say when I thought of him, so slight, so vulnerable, so intelligent. So promising. He made me think of the promising legions of the young gassed by the Nazis. To destroy the promising, how it breaks the heart, whether a wild creature or a human being. And yet it is done.

Quakerism brings one face to face with unarguable truths. It is unambiguous. It has no creeds or sacraments, but what it calls 'testimonies'. These testimonies rose out of what they believe were God's intentions for us. They do not impose them on anyone but they themselves live by them. They meet in silence, but they are allowed to break the silence with something worth saying. Or singing. 'Elected silence, sing to me', wrote the teenaged Gerard Manley Hopkins. And it did – and how!

In the old half of the Meeting House, I sat on the men's half of the bench, facing the gallery, the modern chairs, the echoing past, the Venetian window, the cumulative silence of the ages, trying not to think of words.

JULY

A Time to Wed

JULY. The hillside horses flash their tales, the white cat bakes on the wall, her eyes emerald slits. The oaks haven't the energy to rustle. All is burning and still. Using Roger Deacon's inestimable gift, a lightweight scythe, I have demolished a patch of rough before it seeds. The blue of the big field has turned a heavy green. Invisible larks sing without a stop.

It is Saturday – weddings day. The ancient church shimmers in the heat. The bells ring dizzily. The bride arrives. It is our Pam, on her brother's arm. They are neither young nor old. Just timeless. Ditto the groom. The choir, also neither young nor old, but comfortably settled in the space between these verities, sings 'Jesu, joy of man's desiring', and we all sing, 'Guard us, guide us, keep us, feed us'. It is heartfelt and unimaginably beautiful, with the interior sunshine playing on the bride's slender diadem.

Afterwards, some of us board her brother's restored 1947 bus. Next stop, the Crown. And then, late at night, with Japanese lanterns hanging in the trees and the thatched barns straight out of a Samuel Palmer, a Ruby Wedding party, and all the old friends from near and far at table.

On Sunday, I preach on Time. A scattering of dear ones. It is hardly a tactful subject, I realize, halfway through. But possibly they are thinking of sherry. One must hope for the best. Pam and her husband will now be in the Lake District in the rain. And may be watching it splashing down on Wordsworth's grave, the poet who was 'Surprised by joy – impatient as the wind'. At this moment, thousands of women priests are at their altars to the commonsense of mankind and the glory of God.

But I must concentrate, although the heatwave plays tricks with worship. 'Are you listening at the back there?' Possibly you are in a summer dream that is acceptable to heaven. Who can tell? I think of the dragonflies helicoptering over my ponds, the blazing St John's wort, the children bumping down the farm track on their bikes.

However, Time. My notes look up at me, and in the fierce light are sometimes too bright to read. The cool nave is expectant; for this is its property, to hope for answers. But what is the question? Everyone – myself, the tall columns, the trapped insects, the hymn books – has forgotten.

The Preacher, who has seen it all, done it all, replies as best he can; that is, quite wonderfully. There is a time to make love, and a time not to make love, a time to gather stones, a time to throw them away. He said that, in the multitude of dreams, there are many vanities, and that it is a pleasant thing for the eyes to see the sun.

This beautiful book should be required for Anglican Synods and Vatican Councils – for each one of us. The Preacher had not only done it all, but read it all, and he, exhausted by, shall we say, theology, went in search of the truth or the words given 'by one shepherd'. 'Let us hear the conclusion of the whole matter: Fear God, and keep his commandments, for this is the whole duty of man.'

It is not yet midday when we drive off in glittering cars.

John Clare Enters Poets' Corner

THE ENTRANCE of Ted Hughes to Poets' Corner last week took me back to when he and I, and that remarkable Dean, Michael Mayne, himself a good writer, placed a memorial to John Clare in that crowded spot. After Clare, authors went up on the windows above it: Wilde, Herrick. But Hughes's Welsh tablet found floor space at the feet of T. S. Eliot.

It is an amazing concept, our low Olympus, where visitors are brought to a halt by the sheer splendour of its dust. Poets' Corner began when a young 16th-century scholar found the bones of Geoffrey Chaucer scattered about, and housed them at his own expense in a fine tomb in this aisle. Edmund Spenser's lovely monument soon followed it.

Poets' Corner was pretty full when our greatest rural voice, Clare, went to see it. That he should be in it by what he called his 'right to song' would have been unimaginable. But there he is, up on the wall by Matthew Arnold. Mayne, Hughes, and I put him there on a summer's evening in 1989. The abbey sculptor carved the returning raven with the olive leaf in its beak over Clare's name. Edward Storey wrote:

You were there again,
no longer the shy ploughboy
wondering how you had escaped
from the fields of Northamptonshire,
but as an equal with those men
who had been treated better by posterity –
Wordsworth, Byron, Keats and Tennyson.

Hughes read Clare's 'The Nightingale's Nest', one of the greatest bird poems in the language, and we sang Clare's tragic hymn 'A stranger once did bless the earth', to Surrey. There was a tradition in Clare's village, Helpston, of cutting a summer turf and sticking it with wild flowers and calling it a Midsummer Cushion. So, early in the morning, I cut a turf in my farmhouse garden, and covered it with July flowers, and carried it to Westminster Abbey on the train. It weighed a ton.

The Maynes returned to the Deanery to find it on their draining-board. They carried it to the foot of Clare's memorial. Hughes and his wife, Carol, arrived in the afternoon, and we all had tea.

Hughes and I had met some years before at the Roundhouse, where we gave readings to raise money for Wordsworth's Dove Cottage. Hughes read his own poetry, and I read Thomas Hardy's. Afterwards, he and I had a snack in the ice-cream shop nearby. Now he drew the curtain from Clare's memorial, and we all applauded.

I suppose that being admitted to Poets' Corner is the literary equivalent of entering heaven. Only the Dean of Westminster can let a writer in, and he can be plagued with applicants. I was staying at the Deanery with the Maynes when Michael said: 'How about putting Clare in Poets' Corner?', overwhelming me. For I had only recently been made president of the John Clare Society, and this recognition of him was beyond my hopes and dreams.

But thus it was, Hughes, Mayne, and I, hundreds of people, and the fat Midsummer Cushion, and, as with Hughes's own deserved admission, standing there, marvelling at what we had done.

Empire Christians

TRINITY FIVE gone, and the July sun maintains its precedence. The windows are wide all night, and the old roses begin to fall. Rosa Mundi, York, and Lancaster, and the species which have left my head are adrift. This is the week I fix the water. It is done for one more year. The springs will find their way to the tanks in the roof, and to kettles and baths, plus some expert help from the pump man. The overflow will go towards the dragonflies of August.

At lunch, a line comes up from Reginald Heber's hymn about the saints casting down their golden crowns around the glassy sea. Later, listening in bed to the summer, I think of him and his fate. And how refreshing a hot week in England would have been to him, compared with Calcutta.

He would rather have written poetry in rural England but, reluctantly accepting Calcutta at the third invitation, this see, being virtually all India, would kill him at the age of 43. We had the sense not to ask our friend why such a line should hang around in her Christian subconscious. Perhaps the glitter of the Stour Valley had further polished it up.

Heber had breakfast with Sir Walter Scott at Oxford. 'From Greenland's icy mountains', which we no longer sing, although Heber changed 'savage' to 'heathen', was written for a series of services for the Propagation of the Gospel in Wrexham Church in 1919, when his father-in-law commanded: 'Write something for them to sing in the evening.' Four years later, the youthful bishop was on his way to coral strands.

In his *Journal of a Voyage to India* he wrote: 'Though we were now too far off Ceylon to catch the odours of the land, yet it is, we are assured, perfectly true that such odours are perceptible to a very considerable distance. In the Straits of Malacca a smell like that of a hawthorn hedge is commonly experienced; and from Ceylon, at thirty or forty miles, under certain circumstances, a yet more agreeable scent is inhaled.' Almost a century later, E. M. Forster's wise Mrs Moore would smell trouble as her P&O liner reached the Raj.

India's faiths and Britain's faith would run into confusion. Though not so in Forster's autobiographical *The Hill of Devi*. I think he would have survived Heber's impossible task with a shaking of the head, yet we found him holy, holy. A completely brave young man in his struggle to overturn another holiness while dreaming of hawthorn hedges.

I remember my mother worshipping missionaries. Or shall we say giving them great honour. Some were her friends, and their return 'on furlough' for three months every three years was a thrilling time for her. The mission field was, to her, fertile ground, cultivated in some small way with her prayers, the collecting-box, and her untroubled conviction that there were the heathen and there was us.

Her saint was Sister Joan, who ran a girls' mission school in Ceylon. I never saw this truly wonderful woman, but I don't doubt her goodness, her holy holiness. Her English scholarship and practicality. And the heat! More than that which makes the ancient farmhouse creak at this moment. More than for a week. Roll on the furlough!

'Eden Rock'

LISTENING to *Poetry Please*, I hear a familiar voice. Charles Causley is reading his 'Eden Rock'. And there we still are, sitting on a Cornish cliff, ages ago, and it is being read to me before it goes into a book.

Old grey stones speak hopefully of reunion. Charles's poem regards it as no more than a step. John Bunyan saw it as a brave plunge across the Lethe (the Great Ouse), one which requires all one's courage, so that the trumpets could welcome one on the other side. The trumpet that he heard every curfew was blown by the watchman on Bedford Bridge. It blazed into his cell.

Charles had lost his father when he was still a child, but his invalid mother was cared for by him until his middle-age. Everyone said what a happy release it was for him when she died. This well-meant platitude made him mad. And then, eventually, came 'Eden Rock', a statement about reunion which has changed the entire subject for all of us.

His Lethe is no more than one of those step-across rivulets that thread through the Cornish moors. In 'Eden Rock', such a stream separates him from a family picnic in the 1920s. The scene is not one of glassy streets and singing, but of summer grass, a starched tablecloth, and places for three.

His parents, too, are in their twenties, but he, their son, is an old man – although he won't be when he has taken the little step over the waters of death, to seat himself beside them, and the milk is once more poured from the clean sauce-bottle into the familiar blue cups. And the relationships which meant most to them are quite ordinarily resumed.

He and I wrote to each other spasmodically, and met once a year, usually in Launceston. We would drink beer and talk shop. He had a dry wit. Later, we would find ourselves Michael Mayne's guests at Westminster Deanery.

I would hear him descending from his rest after a long rail journey from Cornwall, blinking through his glasses, his diary crammed with theatre bookings. Because country folk make the most of London.

'Eden Rock' always makes me think of Henry King's reunion poem 'Exequy on his wife'. King was the Archdeacon of Colchester in 1617, and the future Bishop of Chichester. In 1624, his beloved wife Anne died, the mother of their four children. She was 24.

King was devastated, and he assured her 'that I will not fail to meet thee in that hollow vale', and that she must listen as 'my pulse, like a soft drum, beats my approach'. For King, it was all a matter of waiting, and of patience, not of final separation. Anne was buried in Old St Paul's Cathedral, and her tomb would become an inferno in 1666. King himself was buried by his second wife in Chichester Cathedral.

Jesus was once asked by the tricky Sadducees: what happened to subsequent wives in heaven? Or first wives? And to marriage itself? He said that such arrangements did not exist there, only angelic love.

For years, King's first wife was like 'a fled star'. Charles Causley's parents were his fled stars. But they hadn't gone far. 'Come along,' they were saying in the familiar meadow, 'tea is ready.' Not being much of a jumper, he had to take Lethe in his stride.

AUGUST

The Dean Dies

SUMMER RAIN. It falls, not for minutes, but for hours, beating the borders into submission, knocking the hollyhocks for six, dashing the scent from the roses. At first, it leaps up from the hard earth, but soon it penetrates. Its noise is like a distant army or motorway. A few birds cry against it, and the white cat, perversely, lies under a leaky tree with her 'poor me' expression. I listen and watch from a high room, wondering what the dry linseed will make of it. Summer rain, the drenching joy of it.

This is the day when Dean Neil Collings would have bumped down the farm track, unfrocked in his Monday shorts, all prepared for our church crawl. Instead, he is looking back at me from the Obituary page. No more creaking entrances to wonders within, no more ploughman's lunches, no more exclamations at the marvels of Suffolk handiwork as we Pevsnered our way through sacred interiors.

What a lot Neil knew. His cathedral-size exclamations as he read tombs, or looked up on high at clerestories ring in my ears. Where such expeditions were concerned, we were a couple well-matched, unwearying in our interest in architecture and fitments, even down to reading on the hymn board what they sang last Sunday. When looking at an old church, one should first look at its old churchyard. This makes all the difference, I find.

I am not sure that Neil and I did this, and have a feeling that we dashed from his car to the south door, all impatient for its revelations. But it really is odd to see his nice face beaming from the Obituary column. Something wrong here. His last duty at St Edmundsbury was to organize the Royal Maundy, and it was the Queen's kindness to visit him as he lay dying from a brain tumour. It all went off perfectly, of course, though not this death.

Quite my favourite account of the mighty but fallen Abbey at Bury St Edmunds is by M. R. James in his cranky but riveting *Suffolk and Norfolk* (1930), written on the little trains that pleasantly criss-crossed East Anglia before the wretched Beeching got his hands on them. 'We will enter Suffolk from Cambridge by the Newmarket line . . .' And he comes to the shrine of St Edmund not as a supplicant, but an indignant. 'It stood on a rich base of marble, green, and purple, and was in the form of a church without a tower.'

Neil's cathedral was in the form of a church without a tower until, in his brief reign, he oversaw its completion. But M. R. James: St Edmund's shrine 'was made of wood, covered with plates of silver-gilt, a gold cresting on the top, a gold relief of Christ in glory at the western end, figures in niches along the sides: "Very cumbrous to deface," said Henry VIII's Commissioners. Four great candles were perpetually alight. Of all this splendour nothing remains.'

It was near this shrine that, in 1214, Magna Carta was drawn up. And it was also near this grave of a murdered young king that a vast outpatients-of-the-sick crawled and stumbled for centuries in hope of cures, when in fact their remedies grew in the fields.

Angel Hill, the fine space in front of Neil's cathedral, is, said M. R. James, 'As good a thing as England can show.' Sleep on, dear brief Dean, with your panache and goodness still very much alive in this place.

The Restless One

THOUGHT FOR THE DAY varies in its memorability. Some you catch; some you do not. Recently I caught one that recreated a summer's day, Box Brownie and all. It was about losing the nearness of Christ. Particularly in old age. To illustrate this loss, the speaker used a painting by Raphael, *The Madonna of the Pinks*. A handsome Italian woman sits for the great artist, but her son does not. Being a toddler rather than a baby at breast, he has to be kept still, and his mother achieves this by means of a flower.

Ages ago, in a Suffolk meadow, another lady arranges the four of us in a flowery meadow to take our photo. Unlike now, she poses us, a baby sister and three brothers in sailor suits, like a reduced cricket team. One of my brothers is chewing a bit of grass, and the other is, like the Lord, kept from wriggling by a bright object – a bunch of keys.

Tall August plants waver above us. A few yards away, and out of sight, there is a deep pit in which men dig clay for bricks. The men have been to the Western Front and to Gallipoli. The lady's snaps will be sent to Chester to be developed for one-and-sixpence. After the holiday, she will return to London, to our grief; for we love her, although we have long forgotten her name. But the four children go on sitting in the grass for ever, the restless one stilled.

The Lady in the Raphael picture is as close as anyone can get to the Son, and the worshippers in the darkly rich church would have come close because of her. The artist, too, was youthful and beautiful, dying at 37 on Good Friday, the same day he was born.

He was able to reveal in his work the energy that lies in stillness. His mother was heartbroken when they sent him away to be a student, to paint other mothers as the Mother of God, but keeping them human. Like Mary. When Millais painted Jesus as a lad in the carpenter's shop, with grubby feet and workworn hands, the Victorians went wild. But as they said in the synagogue after he had read the lesson so wonderfully, 'Isn't he the carpenter's son?'

And wasn't he the walker? Art tends not to show him striding out, on the move, travelling. But poetry does. One of the reasons we go to church is to catch up with him, since he is so out of sight at home. Liturgy causes us to put a spurt on, as do many 'walking' hymns. We tramp through office, garden, the dreadful afternoon telly, the supermarket, the money, and he is a mere dot in the distance, far, far ahead, undiverted by what diverts us most, and strangely most out of sight when we are in the fast car or train.

The Queen in *Alice in Wonderland* says: 'Now, here, you see, it takes all the running you can do, to keep in the same place.' Religion itself keeps us on the go; yet it can get us nowhere. Often, in our country churches, I talk of John Bunyan (the congregations are tolerant of my heroes), a big man with a slow step who remapped Bedfordshire for Christ and the reading world. 'Come, my Way, my Truth, my Life: Such a way as gives us breath', wrote George Herbert, his near-contemporary, out of puff because of illness.

The Last Harvesters

DAYDREAMING through the first lesson – the Song of Solomon – I suddenly hear the words that I had carved on the tombstone of my friend John Nash: 'The flowers appear on the earth; the time of the singing of birds is come.' And then, in my wandering mind, I recall that other words from this beautiful Hebrew poem would have been carved on many a grave, 'Until the day break and the shadows flee away', and how they are an early acceptance of the cloud of unknowing.

In these days, it is fair to say, and without accusation, that these Sunday readings from the Bible do not ring a bell with most people – not so much because they do not read it at other times as because there now exists a vacuum between most villagers and the fields. Radio and film-makers know far more about flowers and birds than did their ancestors, because of Richard Mabey and Mark Cocker, but they are ignorant when it comes to, say, barley.

David, who is never out of his place at the rear of the church after bell-ringing, is often the lone exemplar of a parishioner who worked our fields all his long life, and a man who was part of them – although, in another direction, I doubt if either he or his friends in the back pew know that they are a continuation of the west-end music that led the services when Thomas Hardy accompanied them with his fiddle. How naturally they catch on to the psalm, how familiarly to the Te Deum.

And what a relief to see them in their places when I announce the processional, which is usually myself and Mike. Or Tim. And then this strong sound from those who can pick up the agricultural imagery of scripture.

This week, I saw a young man cut the barley in the top field.

The barley – which they used to name 'drink-corn' – was short and rustling and cracking as it poured from the ground to the grain-trailer. Everywhere else, the day was silent and still, warm and uneventful. The sky was a dull blue bowl. The solitary reaper's little car was parked by the hedge.

I thought of Boaz and the young widow harvesting the barley at Bethlehem, the house of bread, and the boy with five barley loaves in St John's Gospel – the only reference, I think, to barley in the New Testament. But Boaz and Ruth had a huge part to play in the barley field; for their love would found Jesus's family.

Boaz reaped the field; Ruth gleaned it. In reaping, the sickle had to be put into the barley low, and make a clean cut. But there was no clean gathering of the stalks, and this left room for charity. Enamoured, young farmer Boaz ordered untidy cuts so that this unusual fieldworker could gather rather than glean. It was a heady courtship, aided and abetted by Ruth's mother-in-law.

There is a Victorian window in our church which shows an old married couple themselves being 'harvested' in a cornfield, not a barley field. They had farmed here, and I sometimes walk their fields. The last time, one of them was full of sugar beet.

Barley made the first loaf of the year. It was placed on the altar on 1 August, Lammas Day. Loafmass day. It is a whispering crop, which, when cut, does not journey on in a cloud of dust.

Ian Starsmore's Ladder

HAVING GIVEN myself a month's drift, I find it near-impossible not to drift. Thus I sit in the sun watching the clouds go by, and nursing a selfish cat who drifts when she is not eating. The August sky is stunning. Pink, yellow, and black clouds offer chinks of paradise blue. It is alternately quite hot or rather chilly. The collection of short stories flutter or bake.

I remember an old Japanese custom. Two friends from the city come home for dinner, but first they exchange their office clothes for beautiful robes, and sit in the evening light for an hour, drinking sake. They do not speak. They watch or contemplate clouds, dream, drift. Cloud mountains pass through their vision, cloud silences and shapes run through their heads.

At the little matins which followed the eight-o'clock, I preached on the Woman who was above Rubies, and we sang 'Why do the heathen so furiously rage together' – and, indeed, why do they? It is a rough week.

But David arrives, and splits the logs for winter. They fall apart with silvery chimes. I gather the greengages – something that must be done at the moment before the wasps arrive – and fill the deepfreeze with their lusciously firm softness. Then I write a kind of note on my friend Ian Starsmore's silver sculpture of a ladder which has been set up at Cley before it goes to Norwich Cathedral.

The only mention of a ladder in the Bible is the one in Jacob's dream at Bethel. For all that is said about them in guide books, cathedrals could have been built by height-defying angels. There is a rare sketch of masons at work on a cat's cradle of ladder and scaffolding inside a cathedral during the Middle Ages, swinging about like monkeys, and maybe singing: 'For I will consider thy heavens, Even the works of thy fingers' as they put the finishing touch to the quire. Imagine the ladders of Chartres. The Lord was dead when they brought him down the ladder by the cross.

Thousands were living when they climbed the ladder at the scaffold.

I exchanged my treacherous old wooden ladders for light-as-a-feather aluminium ones. Once upon a time, the oak spokes of a worn-out wagon would be turned into ladder rungs. Waste not, want not. But those flimsy ladders in the dizzy nave, and their frail climbers – Lord, have mercy. How they must have swung around in what was like a stone Big Top. God's acrobatic builders, who were nearer to heaven in more ways than one. Don't look down.

David and I go to Aldeburgh, where I was young. The North Sea slapped the shingle. Yachts tottered on the horizon. Visitors did their best not to be cold. The Victorian houses were gaudy, like toys. We bought fish wet from the sea. Nobody swam. The gulls cried incessantly, and a dozen sat on the Moot Hall and looked north. Sizewell floated far off, a white bubble.

Then home to, eventually, more drift. I contemplate my Scarlet Emperor runner beans as they climb to infinity on the bamboo wigwam as bees visit them. I recall that 'The long, long Sundays after Trinity are with us at last'. The woman who was above rubies would not be idling like this. She would be running her linen shop, bossing her servants, humming one of David's songs. She went to bed late, and rose early. She was 'allus on the goo', as they say in Suffolk.

Bird Garden

BUMPING down the track, we are stopped by a pair of frowning Little Owls. They study us for all of a minute, before vanishing into a ditch. As they go, the afternoon light passes through their feathers.

We are returning from Hadleigh, where we bought new secateurs in Partridges, one of those wonderful hardware shops that sell everything from a pin to a suit of armour. And, of course, we went to see the vast church where the Marian martyr Rowland Taylor taught the Reformation, and Fr Hugh Rose founded the Oxford Movement. No surprise that it is an archiepiscopal peculiar.

Some lads with a white dog, which is being hushed, loll on old sofas. Have they seen the wolf with St Edmund's head in the distant southern chapel? A bench-end shows it being carried by the hair to the saint's body, to which it is united before the funeral, which the wolf attends before returning to his wood.

I have always loved this wide church and wide town with its endless timber-framed houses and terrible-beautiful history. They were harvesting all round. The sun hit the fields with a kind of mockery of our earlier drought commotion, their yield being not half bad.

Back home, it is opening time. I open a bird garden for the Royal Society for the Protection of Birds at Flatford, and also our Royal British Legion vegetable and flower show in the village hall, where the silver cups wait for the winners. Two elderly sisters, the Misses Richardson, now with God, gave the Flatford Wildlife Garden to us. It is within feet of the Stour, and ready for public enlightenment.

I had ridden past it on my bike since boyhood, with no suspicion that these ladies existed, although they sold teas. It would have been close to here that Golding Constable, the artist's brother, who never went out without a gun, shot the 'woodspite' (woodpecker). John Constable needed to have one for the painting he was working on in Charlotte Street.

He was for ever writing home to check flowers and birds for his pictures, to get them right. But he would have been puzzled by a bird garden. Paul Nash called his father's tennis courts and elms at Iver a bird garden, creating these pale and enchanting visions of them. He was by the Stour just before the First World War, painting in moonlight.

At matins and evensong, I turn the Bible birds into a sermon. Ornithologically, they are not at all helpful, having human habits rather than their own. It is as though these prophets and poets had never seen a bird for what it is. And the dreadful sacrificial slaughter, at the Temple, of sparrows and doves. And the tenderness of the Lord. How it continues to break one's heart, this fearful approach to God via blood. How barbaric it was. And did nobody actually watch birds? Surely they must have done. Who could not watch a bird?

I remember John Clare and his birdwatching poems, the greatest in the language, and remember Ted Hughes reading Clare's 'The Nightingale's Nest' in Westminster Abbey, a masterpiece of bird-observation written at a time when 'nesting' by boys of his age was a popular sport, like Golding Constable's pot-shotting as he wandered by the river.

Yet the poetry of poor Job's description of himself as 'a brother to dragons and a companion to owls', how lonely it is. Like my owls calling at night.

'I Feel the Flowers Growing Over Me'

HAVING LUNCH at the art gallery before the lecture, out of the blue, as it were, the old friend mentioned that her great-grandfather was Joseph Severn. On an autumn day in 1820, Severn had boarded the *Maria Crowther* with John Keats in London dock to sail with him to Italy, to nurse him in a milder climate. A few months later the poet would die in his arms.

The lunch continued, but the unexpected information changed it for me. The old friend, an artist like her great-grandfather, had a beautiful old face. Severn drew Keats, read to him from Jeremy Taylor's *Holy Living and Holy Dying*, which is not a depressing book, played to him Haydn sonatas, and had engraved on his tombstone those tragic though misjudged words, 'Here lies one whose name was writ in water.' They were in their twenties.

I had taken matins just before the art gallery lecture and, as well as this Severn connection, I kept recalling the enchanting Psalm 16, which we had sung, about not running after another god and finding 'pleasure for evermore' in the God I possessed.

And then Jeremy gave his lecture on John Nash, an artist each of us had 'possessed' in our different ways. Images of his paintings fell on the screen, watercolours of plants – 'I feel the flowers growing over me,' Keats told Severn – a First World War picture of young soldiers being mown down in the trenches, a wintry oil of my ponds, wood engravings, funny cartoons. Then home to the old farm, meeting the white cat in the black orchard en route.

On Tuesday, David and his collie arrive, each ecstatic in his own way. The collie because he always is, David because his Community Orchard is all settled. 'I need to live another 20 years, that's all, and I will be picking fruit!' He is choosing the apples and pears, the soft fruit, and even the wild daffodils and tulips; for orchards must be carpeted in spring. He is on his way to the head teacher with armfuls of fruit books for the school.

David is infectious. Half an hour in his company, and one is out of the house and into the fields. The Community Orchard has been on his mind for ages. Rare old apples, mysterious old pears such as those the monks pulped. 'All was for an apple', we may soon be singing. Except that all was not.

There are no apples in Genesis, just the fruit of a tree in the middle of the garden. Latin may have been to blame: malus is the word for apple and evil. And then the serpent became a worm, and the worm became a dragon, and natural history became, well . . .

David and I, and the collie, have long ago pulled back from these myths. Our wonders are more lovely and more edible. Our Eden, aka the Community Orchard, will contain D'Arcy Spice, Codlins, and many blessed species that you won't find growing in Sainsbury's. We have a glass of wine to celebrate, and the collie bonks his tail against the chair in joy. Oh, that we may live to gather what we have planted!

There has been a mighty gale, thrilling to crouch under. The house shuddered; the treetops thrashed about; the rain hit the ground running; the noise was terrible. I left the door a fraction ajar to enjoy it. But still the oak leaves hung on, hissing and dripping. The universe was drenched.

David's Community Orchard

THE REMARKABLE day has arrived, at last, at last. I am allowed to see the Community Orchard. It was planted as long ago as February, in two acres of Woodland Trust. And its originator was, of course, my remarkable friend David Baker.

For ages he has talked to me about it, a Community Orchard, one in which local folk can devour local fruit. In our case, Coe's Golden Drop plums, Polstead Black cherries, Johnny Mount pears from Colchester, Sturmer Pippins, D'Arcy Spice apples, and Grey Pippin apples from Mount Bures, one of our parishes.

There they stand, belted to poles. No longer can they escape into obscurity. We will observe them from blossom to fruit, and taste their ancient sweetness. Below them, my wild daffodils – the ones which Dorothy Wordsworth saw, and her brother immortalized – are taking root. Above them, the swallows haphazardly fly about in the cold August evening.

David leads me from tree to tree, making introductions in his eager voice: 'St Edmund's Russet, raised by Mr Harvey at Bury St Edmund's, Suffolk, in about 1875. Sweet, juicy, rich, and densely textured, pale-cream flesh. When really ripe, tastes like pear-flavoured vanilla ice cream. Disappointing if picked too early. Light russet with silvery sheen over with greenish-yellow-gold ground colour.'

He has driven all over England in his van to track down candidates for the Community Orchard, haggling with nurserymen, seeking advice from our next-door apple-guru, the wonderful Andrew Tann, picking up clues about Twining's Pippin. Thomas Twining was the Curate of his parish church in the 18th century, a keen pomologist, and the grandson of the founder of the Twinings tea company. Oh, for more pomologist curates. Oh, for a curate of any apple persuasion – but we must not go into that. Let us be thankful for our David Bakers, naturalists who, with their dogs, leave the beaten path to discover a second countryside, with its stray fruit, forgotten flowers, and neglected glories.

The Community Orchard – it deserves to be named after

him, but he sweeps the suggestion away – is six months old, but in three years it will fruit. Wild tulips and rare grasses will carpet its roots. Wheatears will take a rest in it on their journey to Africa.

'Here', David says in a grave voice, 'is the Isaac Newton tree.' Not the . . . 'Yes,' David says, 'the very one.' It stands stiffly in its rabbit-guard, and is far too short to fall on anyone's head. It has descended from Newton's garden in Woolsthorpe Manor, near Grantham. 'Cooks to a sweet delicately flavoured purée. Large, heavily ribbed.'

David breaks into my worship with, 'I must knock down some of your Victoria plums when we get home, to make some jam.' Here are the Black Polstead cherries. They rose high on Sudbury market-hill when I was a boy; dark, dull, delicious.

Polstead cherries, Polstead cherries,
Red as Maria Marten's blood!

It is astonishingly chill for late August. The hedgerow trees are stock still. We march on. There are 59 members of the Community Orchard, and I must say hello to every one of them. Some would have perished in childbirth had not David nourished them with pond-water during the desert spring. No likelihood of death now, only of constant fruitings. Plus some allowable worship.

Sea Voices

TWO DAYS preparing a programme of John Masefield readings and songs. His all-too-articulate men – for their crushingly repressive time – raise their wild voices. Artisans, seamen, farm labourers, frequently drunk and randy, disturb the peace. The magistrates then were deafened by folk who 'disturbed the peace'.

In 1911, Masefield published his book-length poem 'The Everlasting Mercy', in which his hero, Saul Kane, disturbed the critics. Then came *Dauber*, and an army of young men who articulated an aspect of the British Empire which even Kipling and Wells shunned. Masefield moved from rowdiness to delicacy, from irony to an unmatched evocation of the rough shipping routes and distant murmuring shores.

I found myself checking the veracity of his descriptions of the power of the latter by holding the big conch shell to my ear, as we did as boys, and lo and behold, I heard India's coral strand. Softly rising and falling, Queen Victoria's ocean was still there. And me sitting in the garden with the combine rumbling across the corn.

It was as mesmerising as ever.

The Masefield Merchant Navy heroes brought such shells home, clapped them to their ears when they became restless, then tramped off down to the shipping office, to the relief of their home town. Or something of the sort. He called it 'Sea-Fever'. He himself caught it but once. But it lasted him a lifetime.

It would give him the entrée to a close, often foetid, usually violent male world which poetry had somehow missed. To understand it fully, and as it was at that time, you need to read the 'shipping' Masefield alongside the shipping Conrad. It was where the toilers of the factories and the fields were afloat.

These mid-August days are still. Barely a leaf moves. The old lanes are blocked with harvesters, single toilers in vast vehicles.

They wave like maharajahs under howdahs as I squeeze past. The corn they cut is a foot high. It is like mowing a 50-acre lawn. They go up and down, not round and round, and a panting rabbit or hare is rare. When I think of the carnage when they cut in the old days; the sticks and howls, the bloody Sunday dinner borne home in triumph!

A few birds call above the wheat-dust. For the majority of country people these days, harvesting is little more than a hold-up for cars. In the garden, I listen to the corporate drone of the near and far combines much as I listen to the waves in the conch shell. Each creates reverie.

Standing over the stubble, the friend and I touch on worship preferences. Joyful racket, or a kind of creative silence? While allowing that the Church would most likely die out if it was left to Christians like us, we shrink from those who disturb its peace. By nature we are Anglican quietists, treading softly through the beautiful words, advancing and not purposely going backwards, at ease in the maze known as liturgy, knowingly finding our way about, and happy in these patterns of prayer.

But, as I have confessed before, my trouble is to get occasionally held up when I am taking the service by a sentence of such splendour that it stops me in my tracks. Long ago, it might have been reckoned 'saving words'. And then church architecture tends to butt in. By which time, the congregation is far ahead. Conrad's and Masefield's anti-heroes and loud-mouthers would hear Christ talking, and what a surprise!

SEPTEMBER

Cuts

I AM TAKING my vast bay tree to task when the new window-cleaner arrives. Then come Richard Mabey and Polly; and then the ever-curious white cat. They all eye my destruction as Jonah eyed the fall of Nineveh, that great city. Richard has just written an anti-destructive account of *Weeds*, his new book. All of these watchers know that I am not a destroyer – as, indeed, my garden testifies.

It is a nice, sultry morning for standing about and seeing others toil. Beloved *Laurus nobilis*, I am only doing this for your own good. Your living branches, so tall, so glossy, are they not a shelter for your dead, that brittle forest of sapless sticks which I now tug out with cracking sounds and much dust? Did bay-leaves crown poets, athletes, and Caesars because of their shapely ability to overlay each other, then pointedly describe infinity on their brows? They were hung on the stelae (gravestones) of Olympic winners, where they mouldered for ages.

My bay tree must be all of 40-feet high. Its lower leaves go into the stockpot. I am teaching it to shine, to not become a kind of laurel necropolis. 'I have seen the wicked in great power, spreading himself like a green bay tree', wrote the Psalmist –

which, to some, will suggest the Coalition, no doubt. Society is to be severely trimmed back for its own good. Any minute now, the Damoclean blade will fall, pruning us to the quick.

It is sharpening our wits, however, which the Coalition may not have bargained for. Marches, yes, but an increasingly intellectual response, perhaps not. Even the dreadful banks could be feeling uncomfortable. We are all thinking. I heard the head teacher of an enormous school quietly demolish the argument for cutting out the 'waste' of Special Needs workers, as they were not trained teachers. The head teacher was lucid, formidable, rational, and one of those women who will be making the Education Department slow down on some of its smart-alec policies. The future is certainly scary, but it is also very interesting. Politicians will not find this helpful.

On Saturday, we drove to Saffron Walden, that great town. Although Tim the sculptor and I know the way backwards, we consulted the satnav lady. Not to be made fun of, she took us through every minor road and track she could see from the heavens, and guided us through an Essex so lovely that it left us with a kind of travellers' shock.

With barely another car in sight, and only cyclists doing the September church run, we passed through marvellous villages, took to high and low ground, ducked beneath quiet trees, and glanced at Tudor parks and Celtic earthworks, where we longed to stop and (Tim said) lie in a tent. 'Turn left, turn right,' ordered the satnav lady. Do as I say and all will be well, and all manner of things will be well.

'Supposing we run out of petrol?' I say.

'There's a thought,' Tim says.

We pass Spains Hall, where I once gave a talk, and where the cedars were brought from Lebanon. And then we were in the

Saffron Arms, devouring wine and chicken with all the artists.

'Have you come a long way?' an ancient person enquires. 'Yes,' we say. We are the guests of Richard Bawden, an artist-craftsman, who engraves glass angels and apostles, and paints watercolours, sometimes below my bay tree.

Taking Anne Home to Tannington

ABOUT 40 wild duck screech past the house at about ten to seven each morning in ragged echelon. The September sun is blinding at this hour. The white cat orders breakfast, and girls appear on the hillside to collect their horses.

The days are, well, delicious. One could or should devour them. Bees hang like furry clappers in the fuchsia bells, if this is not a contradiction. My best fuchsia is by the door when it should be in the hedge. I read under it, and fancy it gives a crimson light. Naked ladies in their forbidding purity waver in the border, and there is a smell of rotting fruit.

On Friday, I take the funeral of my neighbour Anne at Tannington, where her farming family lies in tidy rows. Not far away, her horse chomps in his box. He is 39, and the church is filled with riders. This is the part of Suffolk where the Chaucers lived long before *The Canterbury Tales*. I imagine them in the small fields as they manage their oxen and wooden ploughs, careening this way and that, the horizon tilting, scantily clothed, short-lived, this Ethelbert church in the distance.

Anne and I would have ancestral talks on the telephone. The organist's introit is a medley of nice gloomy hymns. As I wait to say 'I am the resurrection and the life' below the tower arch, they collude in ancient sadness. 'Nothing in my hand I bring, Simply to Thy Cross I cling . . .'

Outside, many aunts lie under identical stones. Then to the pub for the funeral meats, everyone handsomely dressed. Do my words ring in their ears, or has the bliss of autumn crossed them out? What a sweet day! What good beer! What a kind old friend, quite gone. One of our similarities was that each of us lived in a little wood that was filled with badgers, foxes, wood-peckers – small 'arks' that shelter creatures from destruction.

Driving back we pass through the old cider country of a Huguenot family, the Chevalliers, whose trucks would trundle through the villages in search of falls, and whose gorgeous drink now heads the best menus. They brought their cider-press with them when they fled from Marie de Medici.

Bernard, who is driving, scans the fields. Not a soul to be seen. Some have been ploughed after the harvest; some harrowed; most are stubbly and waiting. It is mid-afternoon and golden, and very still. Fallen leaves are already collecting in the gutters. Vast clouds.

Who heard my words? 'So teach us to number our days.' This goes for me; for I am somewhat time-illiterate. Cars begin to form processions along the minor roads as workers drive home.

On Sunday, I give our organist Meriel my friend Alan Roth's setting of George Herbert's poem 'The Flower'.

Who could have thought my shrivelled heart could have
    recovered greenness?
It was gone quite underground; as flowers depart
To see their mother root, when they have blown;
Where they together all the hard weather,
Dead to the world, keep house unknown.

We were taught to sing it at Bemerton, but now everyone can learn it from a collection, *Another Music*. Alan actually composed it in Herbert's rectory.

The Damascus Light

EVERY SEASON has its day, its epitome. And this is autumn's apotheosis. It began at dawn, with haphazard yellow streaks which announced sunrise, and it will conclude in rich gold. This much I prophesy.

Ash leaves fall like the Albert Hall poppies, sadly and significantly, alighting on my hair and braking their descent. Huge birds, too, although, only when I go in, a bouncing hen-pheasant and a sprawling green woodpecker who has lost his balance. It is warm, almost sultry, and quite still. Some fields are greening, some doing nothing at all. Just waiting.

Harvest festivals roll into one another. Annette, the Archdeacon, preaches about parched lands while my brook falls musically into my pond.

David and I unearth a crushed granary, get a good fire going, and burn sodden timbers, mats of ivy, and some very strange things that have been mouldering away since Suez. And all the time the blessed autumn day caresses us, calls us, spreads itself out decadently.

We smell of rot, become imprisoned in chicken-wire and, now and then, hold up our finds. A coal-scuttle, good as new, and things that are barely recognizable; for such is existence below a departed shed. Its interior was limewashed against dampness, maybe, for seeds. There are no end of jam jars.

Spiders peer through them. And then the October sun bursts in where it cannot have been for 100 years. We talk divinity.

A stranger calls to bring me a lamp from – Damascus. It seems to be constructed of splintered glass which becomes kaleidoscopic when it is switched on, and very gorgeous, like when one sees through one's eyelids. The white cat stares at it uncertainly. Damascus! Imagine it.

I think of Paul's blindness at the gate, and that demanding voice. It is all I know about Damascus.

I look it up in one of those know-all books. No mention of lamps, but people lived there 1,600 years before Paul arrived with his warrants and was guided to the street called Straight.

Wasps come in after the lamp, game for anything gorgeous. It always takes me a week to like a new thing, and longer than that to love it. What would David like to drink – he having toiled so hard? 'Port,' he says. Port! After supper, we return to the old stackyard to watch the ashes glow. Owls are calling up and down the river. Through the distant window the Damascene lamp is shining like Christmas.

The first lesson for the next evensong is Proverbs 4: 'Wisdom is the principal thing; therefore get Wisdom; and with all thy getting get understanding.' Quite. 'Exalt her, and she shall promote thee.'

The news is dreadfully unwise at the moment – very unexalting. But then, it was unwise of me to stand on a wasps' nest and receive three stings. 'Vinegar,' David says. The stings fade into an itch. More wasps on the wrong side of my bedroom window. I let them out into the smoky darkness.

The owls are hard at it now, and the valley has become a kind of trumpet, funnelling their melancholy hoots into two counties. I dream of poor Captain Naaman of Damascus, being given sick-leave to go to wash away his leprosy in the Jordan, and travelling Paul's road in reverse, and the prophet not even bothering to come out to meet him, and what a ditch compared with the Abana, the Pharpar . . . And most likely owl-ridden.

President of the Kilvert Society

AT EIGHT o'clock in the morning, I go to the orchard in search of breakfast, where the white cat stares at me from a sagging branch. I discover 20 unpecked, or ungnawed, pears. I also discover the following in Francis Kilvert's *Diary*. (As president of his Society, I have to keep up with him.) Alas, the Welsh border is too far away for me to accompany it on its neo-Victorian outings, much as I would like to. But this is what appears in the *Diary* for Tuesday 6 September 1870:

> We went into the green orchard where beautiful waxen-looking August apples lay in the grass, under the heavily loaded trees. Williams gave me a pocket full of apples. The postman came in with the latest news, the *Evening Standard*. Williams tore the paper open and we saw the reports of Saturday confirmed and that a Republic had been proclaimed in Paris under General Trocher.
>
> Crichton sent me 1½ brace of partridges. Really people are very kind in sending me game.

Our postman, Jamie, bumps down the farm track, thin as a rake, infinitely kind, and puts the letters in a glass-covered box which will soon be lost in the undergrowth. Soon, we are to have one of those mailboxes on a pole which one sees in American films. All this to save Jamie a trek to the house.

Listening to Trollope's *The American Senator* on Radio 4 on Sunday afternoon, this visitor to England – at about the same time as Kilvert was writing his *Diary* – deplores the absurdity of the House of Lords, but delights in 'your pillar boxes'. The letter box on the churchyard wall says V.R.

It was probably on New Year's Day 1870 that Kilvert, Curate of Clyro, walked to Hay-on-Wye to purchase his first notebook at Horden's, the stationer's, thus to create one of the most brilliant records of the rural Church of England. Even now, all these years later, no country parish should be without it. It greens the Incumbents Board and sets the registers alive.

Kilvert was 30 when he began his *Diary*. 'Why do I keep this voluminous journal? I can hardly tell. Partly because life appears to me such a curious and wonderful thing, that it almost seems a pity that even such a humble and uneventful life as mine should pass altogether away without some such record as this, and partly because I think the record may amuse and interest some who come after me.'

He was a tall, strong, glossy-haired young priest, who could not be further from the curates who were mocked in *Punch*. He would die, suddenly, at 39.

Kilvert spent a lot of his time at what he called 'villaging', that is, calling. This is what the *Hereford Times* said about his first harvest festival at Clyro: 'Upon the walls between the windows hung St Andrew's crosses of barley sheaves, the butts looped across with wild hop sprays. The chancel wall and west wall were adorned with texts of white letters on a scarlet ground, "Thou visiteth the earth and blesseth it." '

The service was short and hearty. Rare and magnificent ferns lined the altar steps . . . In the font 'a cross of white flowers floated in the water'. The choir sang an anthem by Mr Evans, the schoolmaster, 'with great power, sweetness, and precision'. What more could one ask? My grandparents would have been in their Suffolk village church then.

'The Consolation of Philosophy'

LONG AGO, I worked in a wonderful library. It contained not only the usual stock of reference books and what was called the Local Collection, but a kind of Gentleman's Library from the 18th century, and Archbishop Samuel Harsnett's Library, an eclectic selection of books, among which was *The Consolation of Philosophy* by Boethius, which Chaucer had translated and Caxton had published.

As a young man, I was mesmerized by this beautiful work. It lived in a safe, and was wrapped up in a yellowing copy of *The Times*, and I handled it gently without white cotton gloves. Like some of St Paul's Letters, Malory's *Morte D'Arthur*, and Bunyan's *The Pilgrim's Progress*, it is among the great prison-writings, many of which would not have been written out of prison.

It came to mind the other Sunday morning when, getting ready to take matins, I heard John Gray being philosophical on the radio. He mentioned Michel de Montaigne, of course. And, suddenly, with philosophy in the air, everything became, if not possible, endurable. Children should be taught philosophy at an early age. The old should take to it like honey. Politicians should not only never be without it, but able to speak it.

And then there is this marvellous word 'console'. 'O divine

Master,' begged St Francis of Assisi, 'grant that I may not so much seek to be consoled as to console, to be understood as to understand, to be loved as to love.'

At this moment, I am being consoled by Jim Ede, who knocked together a row of Cambridge cottages and turned them into a perfect art gallery. You ring the bell to enter. Ede sleeps in the shade of a little hilltop redundant church near by, keeping his eye on the Alfred Wallises.

Kettle's Yard is a perfect exercise in modesty, of what one person required in paintings and drawings. The artists who made them were pushing against the limits of their day, and were visionary, or looking ahead. But now we look back on them, and with such gratitude.

Antony and I pass quietly over the brick floors as scudding showers and lances of occasional sunshine break against Ede's windows, looking at everything he found necessary by way of art: the Christopher Woods, the Winifred Nicholsons, the Gaudier-Brzeskas and, of course, a whole fleet of rocking Cornish boats by Alfred Wallis. The pictures are unlabelled; so the visitor, unless he or she reverts to the little guidebook, has to go by pure recognition.

And then, home, to similar brick floors and casements, small treasures and simplicities. And to finding out who Harsnett was – he who added to his mostly Reformation library a sixth-century volume, *The Consolation of Philosophy*.

Well, he was a High Churchman who, in 1628, followed George Montaigne as Archbishop of York, a scholar (and somewhat difficult priest) who loved beauty in worship, and who at that time needed all the philosophy he could get. And who left all his books to his native town, Colchester, so that a 21-year-old could browse among them.

I see him reading Boethius, and being brought to a halt by sentences such as this: 'In every adversity of fortune, to have been happy is the most unhappy kind of misfortune.' Not only Caxton, but Elizabeth I translated this wry masterpiece.

'What Did You Go to See?'

WE ARE having a Bible class, and not before time. It is Saturday morning, and the summer is not quite here, so the church is chilly. The scholarly young priest gives us Mark 10 in Hebrew, Greek, Latin, King James, and New English, through which blind Bartimaeus glimmers into view. Jesus is on his last walk to Jerusalem when this beggar cries out for sight.

We have been told to bring our Bibles, and a fine assortment they are, some pristine, some in tatters. The healer and the healed gradually come into focus. As does, for me, the east window, which I normally sit at right angles to, and do not see. It is brilliant and Christmassy, all gold and green. It makes me realize that to sit in one's place in a church, year after year, with the same piece of it always in view, must shape one's faith to some degree.

But St Mark hurries on. No architectural wandering for him. Youthful, energetic, clear-sighted, he writes the first Gospel. This begins with Christ's baptism and ends with our baptism. As for the now-seeing Bartimaeus, Mark says, simply: 'He followed him in his way.'

Eventually the summer arrives. It loads the white plates of hogweed with glittering insects, and the first dragonflies take off. I scythe a way through the orchard. Roger Deacon gave me this scythe, and it is very nearly my best present. It is made of light metal, and is not at all Father Time-ish, but youthful, like Mark, and cutting-edged. I let the swaths lie and watch the nettles fall like defeated armies. Butterflies muster. The cloudless sky turns sapphire and pink, then deep blue. Self-heal flowers near the potatoes.

A Muslim from Cambridge announces Ramadan, the great fast, and does not mince his words. His colour supplement begins with white obesity and ends with black starvation: people who have waddled to the lager-box, people who have walked many miles for a cup of water. Fasting clears the head, he maintains. Fasting is not starving, however. Nor should eating be more than nourishment and pleasure.

And so to a nice pub that looks out on to the Little Cornard height where Martin Shaw set 'Hills of the North, rejoice.' Fish and chips and no guilt. Below me, the water-meadows of boyhood, with the Stour parting them, and some vague kind of work which was not harvesting going on in them. What are they doing? No answer.

Look close enough into any landscape, and you will find a figure idling or toiling, passing or standing still. And it might find you staring. Jesus was mocking when the solitary figure of his cousin, John, down by the river, drew the crowds. 'What did you go out into the wilderness to look at? A reed shaken by the wind?' John was a fascinating sight; so they went to look at him, not to hear him. Prophets were not sideshows.

Writers do a lot of looking – often more than listening, if the truth be known. The world is so strange to them. They sit at the windows of remote houses, trying to take it all in – the delights and dreadfulness of things, the changing weather, and what it can be to be newly sighted, although not necessarily visionary.

One must not ask too much. Just enough light to walk in the way.

Michaelmas Wakes

THE YEAR is starred with outings. Lengthy grinds at the mill, and then – to Discoed. Which you should be able to find on the map, although with sharp eyes. It is where the poet Edward Storey has invented an annual event, Michaelmas Wakes, and where I have one of those small hoards of friends which are so needful to life.

Two or three days in Powys. East Anglian brightness is exchanged for subdued skies. Kites sail over the motorway early on, but when this gives way to Border lanes, we – there are two of us making the pilgrimage – let go, as it were, and become a different species.

Hospitable Lower Rowley is as lovely as its name, a shepherd's farm tucked into the hills, and amazingly, since rain is never far off, with news of drought and glimpses of shrunken streams. But the Michaelmas trees – what glories! Although what I like most of all when I traipse to another land is its odour, its indefinable essence. It is not something one can take home; so it has to be breathed in at every step, and left behind.

A quintet arrives. Gwylim the churchwarden arrives. So do all the Discoedians, the Readers, the Rector, who, like George Herbert, is now a Prebendary, and the founder of the feast, Edward himself. In between, I snatch pages of Patrick Barkham's *The Butterfly Isles: A Summer in Search of our*

Emperors and Admirals, but do not walk. I sit about, reading, and looking and listening.

This is an astonishing book; it tells one how to get to the Duke of Burgundy fritillary, Small Blue, Adonis Blue, Marbled White, Green Hairstreak, and Dingy Skipper by rail. The quintet plays, among other things, a sonata by Cyril Scott.

Coming home all too soon, we drive over Naseby battlefield (1645), which my American encyclopaedia calls a triumph for the middle class. Countless other cars speed over it too – over the dead, and over the gain and the defeat. We contrive to spin off to the left to Leicestershire, to seek a pub with lunch. When we do, it is to sit in an old bar with everyone watching motor-racing on a big screen. A fine church stands opposite, where it has done for 1,000 years.

'Is everything all right?' asks the landlady.

Somehow, it is; very all right. Earlier on, we found a Welsh-English morning service, and a priest with a good voice, and a Victorian church on a height, and some hymns that we didn't know but soon learnt, and lessons read in the quietest way imaginable, and it sufficed.

A thoughtful soul brushed the rain from my blazer by way of welcome. When the aged St John was pestered for information about Jesus, he would say: 'Little children, love one another.' And, when they protested at his inadequacy, he would add: 'It will suffice.'

The hilly parish was polished black with rain. The latches clicked on our pew, as we let ourselves out. The good sermon spoken from the chancel step was gravely delivered. 'It was', said Rodger, who was a distinguished historian, 'a Norman place.' It was certainly holy where we were concerned. And such good houses, with creepers and fine porches. A wet, shining place, with birds skimming about and with mountains in view and a churchyard like a helter-skelter of graves.

We walked to the car alongside an elderly joiner who had come there from foreign parts in his youth, and it had sufficed. A boy's lunch had once sufficed a crowd. What is going to suffice capitalism at this moment?

OCTOBER

White Cat Stylites

WHAT AN EARLY OCTOBER! I have given myself up to it. Let Robert and Stephanie, the Angels of Mammon, pour out their dire warnings, I cannot understand what they are saying anyway.

I have sat in the sun. I have read poems and books about butterflies. David rang to say that he has been haymaking in Buckinghamshire, and I have crunched over the warm dry mast from my oak trees, picked quinces, and seen the 7.40 flight of the Stour Valley geese.

Harvest Festivals loom. Phyllida will have saved a sheaf from the dusty threshed field to focus our gratitude. Archdeacon Annette will mount our pulpit. There will be an anthem. And God will 'restore the voice of joy and health unto our dwellings'. Thus 'We offer unto thy Divine Majesty the sacrifice of praise and thanksgiving, lauding and magnifying thy glorious Name for such thy preservation and providence over us.'

When the Essex and Suffolk Hunt ran through Bottengoms like a horse-and-hound river, ecstatic, noisy, the white cat took to the trees. Since when she has dozed on a brick pier, gazing down on me with green eyes as I tidy the dying beds, a kind of feline Simeon Stylites, or pillar ascetic.

Simeon started low, but gradually built his pillar up to 40 cubits, and there he sat for years and years, preoccupied with adoration, and looking down on lesser beings. All this in the cause of Chalcedonian orthodoxy. The white cat descends fast at the mere hint of food. Or love. Late roses act as censors.

Friends are terribly ill as their time runs out. They buy plots and choose hymns. The autumn warmth creeps into their rooms. 'It must be nice outside.' Fresh flowers and unread books on the table. 'How about a nice little drink?' Oh, yes. When to arrive, when to leave.

I have been listening to Hildegard of Bingen, her voice as soaring as ever it was after close on 1,000 years. We heard it in an ancient church where it climbed around the Norman brickwork and out into the evening air, the girl singing it rapt and beautiful. Nothing dies, the song says. I was actually sitting below a plaque I had unveiled years ago – but to whom? I have to read it to find out.

Joaquim telephones from Berlin. He is preparing for Yom Kippur, the Day of Atonement. There will be crowds in the synagogue, and fasting, and thrilling singing by the cantor. He sounds happy and busy. He designs gardens and rides a motorbike. What is the weather like? 'Gorgeous.'

I imagine the late sun on the face of the Lord, as he picks and nibbles corn. Corn is instantly understood, but manna means 'What is it?' We walked through prickly harvest fields when we were children in Suffolk. The heat and rough going wore us out. We were not tall enough to walk in this way. 'Catch up!' the grown-ups would cry. We disturbed larks, and the dog crashed ahead.

The church was like a greengrocer's. Nothing merely symbolic. Just 'Plenty'. Grapes swinging from the oil-lamp brackets, apples tumbling, marrows like airships. Brown eggs in hay nests. Home-made wine, elderberry – very heady. And the last congregations to be aching with toil. There was this rich smell of produce, of locality.

Impossible Money

AN AUTUMN morning, very early. The white cat washes herself on one end of the ironing board as I press shirts on the other. The ash leaves have all fallen; so now it is time for the hawthorns to follow suit. Not a mite of wind.

On the radio, Evan Davis, Mammon's angel, is talking to a Mr Warren Buffett, of Oklahoma, who is the world's second-richest man. Mr Buffett lives in a nondescript house with a nondescript car, and there is no computer in his non-descript office. He likes Evan, with his sweet, crocodile grin. Why does Mr Buffett do it, make impossible amounts of money? Evan does not ask. He knows that Mr Buffett does not know why.

I walk in the dank, after-breakfast garden, and smell the lovely rot. Nothing can be done until the trees are bare. A waste of time. Blackbirds scuttle out of berries, geese whoop overhead. I gather some Warden pears for the oven, but let the last roses stay on the wall.

It is the feast day of St Frumentius (I looked him up), a youth who took Christianity to Ethiopia in the fourth century. All true. He and his friend Aedesius got permission for Greek businessmen to set up chapels all over this kingdom. When Frumentius asked for a bishop, St Athanasius made him the bishop. He and Aedesius were most likely teenagers. Mortal spans were brief then, and one did not hang about.

The faith they took to Ethiopia was that of Christian Egypt – the Copts. I see them frescoed on walls, tall elegant young men in classy robes who were taken seriously.

On Bible Sunday, I prayed for translators. And I suggested that it would be a good thing if we each read the Bible at home, as well as from the lectern. Have I not seen them riffling desperately through the pages in search of Amos? Mother would have found him like a shot. What a lot of sacred things there are, what a lot of wicked things! And the travels! Everyone walking miles, like Frumentius and his friend. And the poetry – how divine!

Here is St James on money in William Tyndale's translation:

'Go to now ye rich men. Weep, and howl on your wretchedness that shall come upon you. Your riches is corrupt, your garments are moth-eaten. Your gold and your silver are cankered, and the rust of them shall be a witness unto you, and shall eat your flesh as it were fire.'

Today we touch coin only for small things, when once it was touched for everything – although I dare say that Mr Buffett still understands the need for small change, embarrassing though it can be: nothing rolls as far as a penny in church.

Like everyone else, I sit in luxury to observe the naked and the hungry, while the banks we have saved with public money give huge presents to themselves. Where Christ went on about materialism, the Church goes on about sex and gender – things that little interested him.

Outside, the golden time is here, each yellow leaf a payment for the summer. 'Let us go into such a city and continue there a year and buy and sell, and win: and yet cannot tell what shall happen tomorrow. For what thing is your life?' Tyndale after St James.

Just two more days of October for me. Then all the saints, most of them broke. And the lovely autumn passing.

The Cornfield Ancestors

ASH LEAVES fall first. They sail down from the mother-tree and spatter the grass. It is moist and mild. A delectable October day. I have come in from sorting out the yuccas whose 'Spanish sabres' stand guard against guests. But how handsome they are as they give grandeur to the garden! When I saw the dead heads from the main stem, it is like cutting through a pineapple, juicy and soft. Blessed rain is in the offing, they say.

Harvest festivals succeed each other in the three parishes, which means variations on the same sermon, as some people attend each one. Thus I try to change the theme of the book of Ruth, which was obviously written by Thomas Hardy. It proves that Jesus's family originated in a cornfield.

Ruth's declaration to her mother-in-law is a perfect way for anyone to state his fidelity to Christ, and, I would like to think, prophetic. '"Whither thou goest, I will go, and where thou lodgest, I will lodge: thy people shall be my people, and thy God, my God" . . . So they two went until they came to Bethlehem.' Which means 'house of bread'.

'Do not forget to put a loaf on the altar,' I unnecessarily instruct the harvest-festival ladies; for they forget nothing. Our harvest is, of course, long past, and next year's wheat is in. The Big Field darkens in the rain. Snowy gulls quarrel over it. The white cat sits in the hedge, keeping dry.

Judith arrives to interview me for her magazine *Waves*, because I helped to judge East Anglia's version of the Booker. She is late, Bottengoms being notoriously hard to find. When she asked a van-man the way to Wormingford, he said: 'Who could tell you?' Or something like that.

She filled up minute pages, took photos, and sipped hot water and lemon, as I tried to say something original about my life. We walked round the bedraggled grounds, and I remembered how, long ago, I had helped judge the Booker Prize itself. William Golding had won it – £10,000 in those days – with his sailing-ship novel *Rights of Passage*. I remembered how he had looked rather like an old ship's captain, with his whiskers and blue eyes.

It was about an 1830s voyage to Australia, and a passenger list that should not have been investigated. When it was – well! Not the least wonderful thing about his novel was Golding's ability to stay in period where the seamanship was concerned. Never a task, never an order, that was informed by modern navigation. When I praised him for this as we stood at the bar, he twinkled. His wife shook her head. Novelists' wives, or husbands, often shake their heads. It is among their necessary functions.

As for ships, a number of them voyage about in my imagination. One was a fishing boat on Galilee in a very bad painting that held my attention in Sunday school. Another is in a marvellous etching by Francis Unwin which hangs before me at this minute, a clipper in full sail; another in R. L. Stevenson's *Letters*.

I have been, in a way, a passenger on these vessels. I still am. Flight has destroyed travel. We must pass through climates and time-zones that touch our flesh if we are to travel. Flight does not allow this.

'I have You in My Heart'

IT IS TOO BEAUTIFUL to work. They said that the sun would shine, but not like this. Deciduous shapes wander down, palmate, cusped, linear, ovate, pinnatifid, and settle on my hair. The warm October sun touches each one. The white cat sits on me, rumbling like a tractor.

'But,' my head reminds me, 'you have to go to Wales to tell them about George Borrow and his *Wild Wales*. And join in the celebrations for the mended church. And meet old friends, some of whom have been dreadfully ill. And take stock of Offa's Dyke.' Time enough. Luke has seduced me with his warm spell.

Only last night it was heavy rain, so that the Vicar had to splash down the track to take me to the PCC, though not cold. As ever, I was amazed by the mixed abilities of its members, their expertise on practically everything. Wild weather beat on the windows. Future services stretched away to kingdom come.

But now, this golden day, with the blackened seed-heads popping and the horses wearing their bright blankets, and the dog-walkers waving. I imagine Commander Aurelius Bassus, from Camulodunum up the road, collecting his wife and children and saying: 'Come on: tie on your sandals. Let's walk west to that nice humpy valley up the road. It is far too nice to rule Britain.'

I see them now and then, the old idlers in my fields, cutting a hazel switch, shouting at crows, or just spread out in the year's final heat, never for one moment realizing that they are historical. No one does. We can accept wars and commerce and dates, but it takes an effort to see a ploughman's autumn face in, say, 1638, and find it to be our own face in the present sunshine.

The arborist has been called in to give, we hope, a clean bill to our churchyard trees. They were planted by a clergyman in the 1890s, and lend splendour to the river approach to the village. Hedgerow oaks of great antiquity add to the fine scene. We await the verdict with bated breath. If all is not totally well, all is far from hopeless. The acer leaning towards the tower has to be watched; the glorious horse chestnuts have dark patches – but not to worry.

Removing a great tree can leave the kind of space caused by demolishing a house. One of lost habitation. A buddleia perched on the north wall, however, cannot stay. And we have a water-butt instead of a tap for the grave flowers, although bottles of spring water in the vestry for sacred purposes, of course. The Stour flashes below. A little girl's grave is a toy-box, and is animated with plastic windmills.

On Trinity 22, I preach on glimpses of the Spirit, how people show them without knowing it. We are to ask God to keep his household the Church in continual godliness. The epistle has Paul telling the Philippians: 'I thank my God upon every remembrance of you', and that 'I have you in my heart.' How grateful this is; how moving.

What happened to him in Philippi, his first European church, to draw such affection from him? He and they exchange 'joy'. In the practical sense, they helped him during his imprisonment. In every other way, he and these proto- 'Christians', like the friends in Antioch, have lifted one another's spirits, and a great love travels between them.

The Spirit is common among us, but never commonplace. We see him on televised faces, their owners having no idea that he shows himself. On the sleeping face in the train. Or on Rembrandt's many faces.

Apples and Plunderers

I AM at the mercy of two great apple-fanciers. They spread their glories before my uncomprehending eyes or, rather, my equally uninformed palate. Try as I must, I can never get much further than telling a cooker from an eater.

Yesterday, John arrived from Letheringham (about which more anon) with a veritable brain-and-tongue-staggering basket of apples which he laid reverently before me, announcing each variety slowly and patiently. I put on my best face as he introduced each one like guests entering a ballroom.

'Howgate Wonder, 1850, a big cooker from the Isle of Wight. American Mother, an eater from Massachusetts. Calville Blanc d'Hiver, 1600, a small pale-green cooker from Paris – a French-tart apple.' And Falstaff, a modern James Grieve apple from Kent, which John's neighbour Polly ffitch had sent me. After he had made his way up the darkening track, I cored and slit a mighty Howgate Wonder, and baked it. The half had not been told me, as the Queen of Sheba said. It was marvellous.

Now for Letheringham, a tiny priory once on my walk-route when I lived in East Suffolk. It lay in Mr Kerr's farmyard, safe at last from the vandals who had pillaged it for generations. It is forgotten that once the official iconoclasts had done their work, the locals moved in for the pickings. Hence, in particular, the stripping out of valuable brass. The Cromwells, Thomas and Oliver, a century apart, are commonly blamed for the 'cleansing' of these medieval buildings, but once they lost their sanctity in the eyes of the community, much of the desecration that we see today was achieved by anyone in the village who needed a bit of this or that.

One of my most beloved books when I was a boy was H. Munro Cautley's *Suffolk Churches and Their Treasures* (1937). He had gone to work in our diocesan surveyor's office in Ipswich, not long after the first Dilapidations Act had been passed in 1871. This is what he discovered at poor Letheringham:

> This little church which has lost its chancel has been terribly treated . . . Of the numerous and splendid brasses of which there is such ample evidence, only one remains, Sir John de Wyngefeld, 1389 . . . Other brasses reaved from this church are in private possession still. Two mutilated figures from the destroyed Wingfield monument have been rescued from the Hall gardens, where they had been taken as ornaments. Apparently one hundred years ago every collector pillaged this church, and some of them were the neighbouring clergy!

And I discovered that a Georgian farmer had broken up the recumbent knights and ladies to fill in his potholes.

Yet from afar – that is, from the lane to Framlingham, and from my dear simple Hoo – Letheringham Priory continues to display what those looters could not take away from it, some essence of the Age of Faith, as they now call it. Now and then a rescued hymn from this age shocks with its accusative language.

> Who was the guilty? Who brought this upon Thee?
> Alas, my treason, Jesu, hath undone thee.

Selwyn College

THE SECOND summer ceases, the leaves splatter on the grass, the clocks go back. The world stands still. It is locked in concepts that no longer work. The international young speak another language into their phones. The politicians have theirs written for them – often over and over again to get it right. Which it rarely is.

The comedy of the party conference becomes less amusing. Voltaire's world was crazy enough, heaven knows. Did his anti-hero advocate escapism when he told us to turn our backs on it and work in the garden? Far from it. He was telling us to do something useful, to be quiet, to think.

Meanwhile, Mammon is in confusion here and now, just as it was for Candide, who also said: 'Optimism is a mania for maintaining that all is well when things are going badly.' The youthful encampments at the centre of capital cities are far ahead of anything the speechwriters can produce. I think of Jesus on the road.

And I am not cut off from thought when I bring the tender plants inside; for the warmth has gone and a crispness is in the air. I retire them to the brick-lined larder, where ropes of onions dangle from hooks and where, through a north window, they can watch the valley.

This year's plum jam shines on the shelf. Generations of preserves have come and gone, but have left their smell. It is both sumptuous and deathly. Friends breathe it in; for it is not something you will find in today's fridge, but Proustian in its power to return the past. Apples lie in regimental rows. Some will rot; some will last.

Family heirlooms, such as Mother's scales, sit on a droopy

shelf. The white cat prances aloft on whitewashed beams – not, I trust, smelling a mouse. Spiders are about. I think of the tent statement being made on the steps of St Paul's Cathedral, the intelligent tent-dwellers, the eloquence of what is being said without speaking. To misquote what Wren's son said of his father: 'If you would see what men have done to the economy, look around.'

A tented encampment in the City – all the great cities – the accusing young faces. What a sight! One to take home with you on the train. And as for all those wildly extravagant ministerial trips, might not the business be done on the screen? What we have been witnessing seems less wicked than ridiculous, a kind of theatre of the absurd.

Last Sunday, I went to Selwyn College, Cambridge, to preach on the Saxon saints at choral evensong. Utterly beautiful. I talked about the Fens' being our 'desert', and about Sylvia Townsend Warner's novel *The Corner That Held Them*, in which three medieval women escape the attentions of illiterate knights to found a cell – as in the seventh century had St Etheldreda, who chose a slight eminence called the Isle of Eels.

The choir sang a Bruckner introit, and we sang 'Christ is made the sure foundation', and I imagined the youthful George Selwyn sailing to New Zealand to take the Church of England to the Maoris, and learning their language en route.

My point was to underline the reality of their patron saint to the young worshippers; for Saxon women with somehow vague names have a way of retreating into the shadows. If you would see her monument, look at Ely Cathedral.

Carl – and Cluny

EVERY NOW and then, the Australian relations arrive. They are young and, quite rightly, I am a duty call before they fly home. Carl and his wife are in their twenties, quite beautiful, and have read economics at Sydney. I take them to the Stour, where his grandmother and I, as children, fished, wandered, drank Tizer. They look at the water dubiously. A river? I apologise, and tell them that it widens a bit at Harwich.

They tell me how they live in the Boathouse. Where else could a Hungarian-Suffolk and a Mauritian-Suffolk couple live? The Boathouse has a landing-stage on Yowie Bay, from which you can sail upstream, turn left, and arrive where Captain Cook landed. You are not supposed to live in boathouses but, of course, you do. You would be mad not to. Australians are not so much law-breakers as law-forgetters.

And anyway, boathouses were invented to give homes to perfect couples. The one thing you must not do in New South Wales is take down a tree. Don't think that the local government hasn't got a photo of your trees.

And what about the money crisis, the one that fills our ears and eyes every minute of the day? The golden boy and girl are politely puzzled. They have been touring Europe for only two months; have they missed something? And then I remember how the old, or fairly old, feed on crises, and the young, or wonderfully youthful, try not to clutter themselves with the news.

I show Carl a photo of his great-grandfather back home from Gallipoli, and mention the terrible wipe-out of the Aussies. The lad in the picture-frame stares back at him.

The next morning, I watch the day break, as usual. The horses on the hill graze into view. The night retreats. Plum-coloured clouds chase it away. The horses are groupies, but they never touch – simply lower their heavy heads to feed. Their tails become spun glass. I imagine Carl in his Sydney tower, the blue harbour, the memory of rural Hungary, from which his teenage father walked to Paris during the revolution, Stalin's tanks. Brief calls leave everything unsaid.

It is Last after Trinity, which means that All Saints' and All Souls' are on the doorstep. The living and the dead will come into the church in a kind of procession. We shall hear their names. Don, bell-ringer, verger, chorister, will have just made it. His name will have arrived before his funeral.

All Souls' was the invention of Odilo of Cluny. It began with an observance at Cluny Abbey itself, and soon spread to the entire Western Church. Odilo, too, was a great traveller. At Cluny, he created something known as the Truce of God, in which armies had to suspend hostilities between Saturday night and Monday morning.

But, also, there was this sad calling of the recent dead into their old places in church. Thus a huge congregation. Here we shall listen to Lamentations: 'They are new every morning: great is thy faithfulness. The Lord if my portion, says my soul; therefore will I hope in him . . . 'It is good that a man should both hope and quietly wait . . . it is good for a man that he should bear the yoke in his youth . . . Let us search and try our ways.'

The dead listen attentively. Lamentations is an ancient dirge, but we get its drift. It fits our sorrow. Garish flowers lie on the graves. Shrivelled leaves blow about. Villagers were laid here before Cluny. A bell rang. Rooks crowded. A surface was disturbed. I read family names. How remote they have become, and so soon.

The First English Hymn

A RIVER-LINE defines the territory of our local saints, Edmund and Cedd, both youthful, one a king, one a bishop. This time, it is the latter's turn for a visit. The day is dull, even sullen. The North Sea is barely visible from the flat land. Two lights a mile or two apart, one physical, the other spiritual, those of Bradwell Nuclear Power Station (1962) and the chapel of St Peter-on-the-Wall (654) show us the way. Wild flowers, scabious, lady's bedstraw, and lady's slipper, edge the wheat.

A dozen of us make these pilgrimages now and then, locking the cars, wandering on, wondering what we will find. Laurence and Margaret, the local priests, come too. The elementary shape draws us on – the pitched roof, the pale design.

St Cedd built it from the stones of Othona, a fort belonging to *The Count of the Saxon Shore*, a boyhood friend of mine. We are now in history with a vengeance, even if what we see is no more than a rough sketch of the past. We grow quiet, although now and then an important question is asked: 'Why is there no restharrow?'

We enter Cedd's cathedral-monastery-university, his Lindisfarne-in-Essex, and settle down. 'Settle down!' our schoolmaster would shout. Here, a vast quiet engulfs us as I strew nightlights along the altar, and robe.

Meriel has printed out my Celtic liturgy, which starts with the Taizé office for noon: 'Sanctify our souls and our bodies.' The chapel smells as fresh as the footpath, it being climatic inside and out, and our shoes being damp with pollen. The prayers are by Alcuin of York:

One goodness ruleth by its single will
All things that are, and have been, and shall be,
Itself abiding, knowing naught of change.

Cedd and his three brothers were Saxon pupils at Lindisfarne who were sent to convert their own people. He arrived here by ship; shrank, it would seem, from the great forest that was Essex; and made his headquarters where he could worship in unison with the noise of the shore. He wore the Celtish tonsure, lopped at the front and long at the back. He taught under oaks, and might have stayed here for ever, had not Rome commanded him to go to the synod as an interpreter; for then, as now, church language is a puzzle to the common man.

The synod was held in Whitby in 664, and was presided over by the formidable Abbess Hild, spending much of its time debating the date of Easter – which would have bored the Celts, as every Sunday was Easter to them.

Here, I had to cease my teaching and continue my prayer; for nothing destroys worship as too much information. Unseen, but felt, the huge stone blocks on every side said Quiet.

But we did sing – quite marvellously, I thought – 'Great is thy faithfulness, O God my Father', standing up and swelling out with gratitude. Or so I thought.

The first English hymn was sung at Whitby. An old herdsman named Caedmon lived there, and was famous for slipping out of the house when the singing began. 'I don't sing.' One night, a voice whispered: 'Caedmon, sing something to me.'

'What shall I sing?'

'Sing the beginning of created things.'

And he did. This is what he sang – the first English hymn. Abbess Hild joined in.

Now we must praise the Ruler of Heaven,
The might of the Lord and his purpose of mind,
The work of the Glorious Father, for He,
God Eternal, established each wonder,
He, Holy Creator, first fashioned the heavens
As a roof for the children of earth,
And then our Guardian, the Everlasting Lord,
Adorned this middle-earth for men.
Praise the Almighty King of Heaven.

Adorned it with seagulls, restharrow, and useful stones, crashing tides and East Anglian skies. And Yorkshire fells, of course.

NOVEMBER

How it Happened

THE REMEMBRANCE once more. There is a palpable element in this annual grief. It announces its arrival in the bare trees, in the dawn skies. I find that a leaf, sailing down from the stripped ash, becomes a poppy petal on the brow of a teenage soldier in the Albert Hall.

Long ago, the Westminster Abbey librarian, Mr Tanner, described to me the burial of the Unknown Warrior, at which he had been present. All this came back to me, as it were, because the artist who had painted Harry Patch had come to stay, and I was telling him about this conversation.

Harry was 107, and had spent much of his life trying to get the trenches out of his head. His longevity was to fix both the war and himself together for ever. The world stared at the thin old man on the screen, still breathing, still speaking. The Unknown Warrior, explained Mr Tanner, was the idea of a young padre, the Revd David Railton, who would later become Vicar of Margate.

After the Armistice, after the millions of 'the fallen', as the poets of the time liked to call them, cried out, like Dido, 'Remember me!', the question was: 'How?' How did a nation remember such an unprecedented slaughter? And then, said Mr Tanner, came this extraordinary suggestion from someone who had been in the thick of it all.

141

One evening, in 1916, wrote the padre,
I came back from the line at dusk. We had just laid to rest
the mortal remains of a comrade. I went to a billet in front of
Erkingham, near Armentières. At the back of the billet was a
small garden, and in the garden, only six paces from the
house, there was a grave. At the head of the grave there stood
a rough cross of white wood. On the cross was written in
deep black-pencilled letters, 'An Unknown British Soldier',
and, in brackets beneath, 'of the Black Watch'. It was dusk,
and no one was near, except some officers in the billet,
playing cards. I can remember how still it was. Even the guns
seemed to be resting.

Now that grave caused me to think. Later on, I nearly
wrote to Sir Douglas Haig to ask if the body of an 'unknown'
comrade might be sent home. I returned to Folkestone in
1919. The mind of the world was in fever. Eventually, I wrote
to Bishop Ryle, the Dean of Westminster . . .

The only request that the noble Dean did not see his way
to grant was the suggestion I gave him – from a relative of
mine – that the tomb should be inscribed as that of the
Unknown Comrade – rather than Warrior . . .

The celebrated text on the grave, 'They buried him among the
Kings because he had done good toward God and toward his
House', had already been in use on an Abbey tomb for almost
600 years, though the Dean did not know it, because he said
that he was indebted to a north-country archdeacon for it. But
Richard II had had it inscribed on the tomb of his friend the
Bishop of Salisbury in 1395.

At first, George V shrank from the suggestion of this
anonymous body arriving at the Abbey. It was novel, and could

be sensational. 'His Majesty is inclined to think that nearly two years after the last shot was fired . . . a funeral might now be regarded as belated, and almost, as it were, reopen the war wound which time is gradually healing.'

Remembrance does not seek to heal.

Reading Aloud

AT SCHOOL, we had Silent Reading and Reading Aloud. Most of this was done from a primer, *Tales the Letters Tell*. A girl named Enid was good at both and would go far, they said. She became a cashier in Barclays Bank, and she would give me a wintry smile, her glasses glittering. I can hear her still as she sailed through the hard words. My downfall was Fast Reading.

'Please, Miss, I've finished.'

'Then start again.'

Soon, *Tales the Letters Tell* would tell me nothing, as boredom set in.

As the old artist and his wife settled by the coal fire after dinner, I would read on. Chapter six of *The Shrimp and the Anemone*. Their eyes closed, and they breathed regularly. 'What are you stopping for?' Their Silent Reading was green Penguin whodunits. I, of course, was reading Proust. I tried him out on them one evening, and they said, 'Oh, very funny.'

The other week I listened to David Holt reading a William Boyd novel that was not quite my cup of tea, but the reading voice was so charming, so right, that I was filled with pleasure.

Jesus caused quite a stir when he read the lesson for the first time at the Nazareth synagogue. It was so beautiful. Where did he get it from – I mean his being, well, the carpenter's son?

There followed some home truths, and they ran him out of town. He had read from Isaiah: 'The Spirit of the Lord is upon me because he hath anointed me to preach the gospel to the poor, to heal the broken-hearted . . .' If only he had left it at that. If only he had not gone on, why, the place would be packed every Saturday.

My favourite Reading Aloud story is the one about the poet Jeremiah getting his bad news to the King. King Jehoiakim was young and happy and was in no mood for bad news. Jeremiah was young and unhappy because he had learnt that Jerusalem was next on the Babylonian conquest list, and because no one would listen to him.

It was not much help that he had 'a beautiful voice'. The only way to get through to his people was to write his warning down. But then, even more beautiful than his voice was his prose style as he dictated his warning to a scribe, Barach, a man who had access to the King.

It was winter, and Jehoiakim was in his winter palace, sitting by a cosy brazier. 'Read the roll to me,' he said. And as the bad news unrolled, he cut off its dire realities with a penknife and threw them into the fire.

The bishops attempted to cut off Tyndale's Bible by throwing it into the bonfire; and the first thing the Nazis did was to burn books.

Society mocked Jeremiah. 'You are no more than a singer of fine songs with a lovely voice,' they said. He wrote: 'All is well. All well? Nothing is well.' Much later, a woman would write, 'All manner of things shall be well.'

Church Music

EARLY MORNING just before Advent, with the dawn making the most of it. A bright yellow wedge prises the fields from the sky, and there is a glimpse of countless crazy birds, then a retreat into darkness.

The white cat sprawls on me as I drink tea and contemplate St Cecilia, who 'sang in her heart to God', who was martyred in the third century, and who has a church named after her in the Trastevere in Rome. In spite of all this, she more or less disappeared until the 17th century, when John Dryden's 'A Song for St Cecilia's Day', 1687, returned her with delightful panache.

The poem praises each instrument in turn – trumpet, flute, drum, violin, and finally organ, possibly suggesting Britten's *Young Person's Guide to the Orchestra*. St Cecilia's Day was his birthday.

Watching the morning, I think of us walking on the marshes with the blue-black Aldeburgh sea thudding on the shingle, all this a long time ago. Dryden said that Cecilia raised music higher than Orpheus, the latter being a pagan. But then he had only a lyre: she was able to pull all the stops out.

I preach on church music on the feast of Christ the King, and read the psalm that he and his friends sang in the upper room, 'When Israel came out of Egypt . . . and the Lord turned the hard rock into a standing water, and the flint-stone into a springing well.' The latter is more or less what we still do ecologically at Wormingford. I also read George Herbert's enchanting 'Church Musick', that 'sweetest of sweets' which he helped to make in Salisbury Cathedral every Thursday.

On the radio, Colm Tóibin's musical voice attempts to philosophize on the Irish dilemma – which makes a change from Stephanie's fiscal hauteur and Evan's wicked grin. The great novelist puts his own spin on what his nation has been up to in good times and bad, and it is as acceptable as all the other remedies. And nicer to listen to.

The Irish use language so beguilingly, so seductively. That building spree! That finding the cupboard bare! Well, what can you do about it, whatever? What'll you have? He brings in Henry James, who never earned much, but did well. What is beyond doubt is that the incessant money-talk of the present time is wrecking life, and that something must be found to put it in its place. If our lives are not to be half-lives, that is.

Jesus put money in its place, and coolly. As did Matthew when he descended from the Customs and Excise. There is an aldermanic tomb in a church near here that declares that its owner, being both laden with goods and charitable, passed through the eye of a needle. As must have done the builders of our wool churches. It was (sacred) economics, stupid.

I found a marvellous music hymn by F. Pratt Green, but, alas! we did not know it. Now here was someone who sang to God in his heart. He once drove me to a poetry society in Norwich. In his hymn 'When, in our music, God is glorified', he reminds us of that scarcely-to-be-imagined fact, Christ singing. It would have been a beautiful voice from, maybe, Temple training. And it would have been heard more than once, but no one recorded it. 'And did not Jesus sing a psalm that night . . . ?'

'Furrows, be Glad!'

ADVENT. Season of name-giving – and such names! Who giveth these names? Heaven only knows. Poets, saints, youths, ancient folk. What shall we call him? Adonaï – a name for God? Dayspring bright? Desire of nations? Key which opens what cannot be closed? Emmanuel, of course.

In the congregation, a baby is long overdue, spinning out womb-days in order to have an Advent birth. What shall we call him or her? Something beautiful. No flowers in church, but all this name-calling. Outside, murk and final sunshine, slippery leaves, and noisy rooks. Inside, I say the sublime Advent collect, the one about putting away works of darkness and putting on the armour of light. Shall we sing Eleanor Farjeon's carol of the Advent?

> Furrows, be glad. Though earth is bare,
> One more seed is planted there:
> Give up your strength the seed to nourish,
> That in course the flower may flourish.
> People, look east, and sing today:
> Love the Rose is on the way.

Quite a lot of charlock is being grown, and brassy yellow alternates with rich browns in the landscape. Trees and hedges are semi-bare, but the air has a sultriness tinged with frost. Norfolk friends are held up by fogs. The white cat takes up winter quarters, this time on my garden-tools table in the boiler room, her tail wound around a hot pipe. She sleeps deeply 23 hours a day and, apart from six square meals, will not come to until late March. Who would?

I would, for one. I would not mind missing Christmas, but to miss Advent! Ages ago, Advent was as strict a fast as Lent, the Second Coming in mind. Now, a confusion of natural and supernatural birth, plus this intense welcoming of the gloriously named Child, plus, it has to be said, an absence of judgemental terror and awe, makes the severity of a flowerless sanctuary a liturgical pointer to winter. Little more.

Richard Mabey arrives, and we talk shop. The years of our friendship are quite amazing. We go back a bit, as they say. We sit by the stove, and the ash logs spit at us. A chicken sizzles in the oven. He and Polly have brought champagne and apple tart. Thus we slummock in the old room as the light fails, careful not to bore one another with current toil, the flames illuminating our three faces.

Polly has returned from Zambia, and from an encouraging account of her son's refrigerator, its hairy contents, and its almost archaeological sell-by dates. Her son runs a wild-animal reserve, and an elephant can, literally, be in the room.

But pythons, tigers – what are these to her son's fearful groceries, mouldering away in the icy darkness? When they have gone, I find some pâté right at the back of my fridge; quite good, but dated 2009. Oh, the waste, the strength of character needed to cast it forth! The fridge stands in a brick-floored dairy, so cold in itself as to compete with this newfangled gadget for keeping food edible for ages. Though not for ever.

Apart from Adonaï-Dayspring-Desire of Nations, what else will Advent bring us? There will be Gaudete Sunday, when, as in mid-Lent, a rose-coloured vestment may be worn. For me, the pulsating season itself will always be enough.

DECEMBER

Carol – to Dance in a Ring

WITH MAMMON on the rampage, I consider the Advent carol. The sun stares down on the cold garden, and bullfinches rock my new feeder. Before me lies a treasured inheritance, *The Oxford Book of Carols*, by Percy Dearmer, R. Vaughan Williams, and Martin Shaw.

I met Martin Shaw when I was a youth. He was my friend Jane Garrett's uncle, as, of course, was his brother Geoffrey, who got John Ireland to set the wonderful hymn 'My song is Love unknown'. So when it comes to the Advent carol service at Little Horkesley, as it does without fail each year, I feel on personal terms with it.

There are six Advent carols in the Oxford book, five of them set by Martin Shaw: 'All hail to the days', 'If ye would hear the angels sing', 'People, look east', 'When Caesar Augustus had raised a taxation', and 'When righteous Joseph wedded was'.

Percy Dearmer (who married my friend Jane's parents) wrote the preface to *The Oxford Book of Carols*, and very fine it is. Everyone arranging this season's Festival of Nine Lessons and Carols should read it. It begins:

Carols are songs with a religious impulse that are simple,

149

hilarious, popular and modern . . . Carol literature and music are rich in true folk-poetry and remain fresh and buoyant even when the subject is a grave one . . .

The word 'carol' has a dancing origin and once meant to dance in a ring . . . it dances because it is so Christian . . . Carols, moreover, were always modern, expressing the manner in which the ordinary man at his best understood the ideas of his age.

Reading this, I recall something from Parson Woodforde's *Diary*. At the end of the Christmas Day service, the people asked if they might sing a carol. 'Not until I am out of the church', said he. This in the 1780s. His *Diary* is full of food, and should be the telly chefs' bible.

But back to Martin Shaw, and his inclusion of Advent carols in the Oxford book, which do not include his setting of 'Hills of the North, rejoice', with its grand geography, so distant from the snug hearth of his:

This time of the year is spent in good cheer,
And neighbours together do meet,
To sit by the fire, with friendly desire,
Each other in love to greet,
Old grudges forgot are put in the pot . . .

He found this in a black-letter tome in the Pepys Library. But the gifted Eleanor Farjeon wrote 'People, look east', with its 'Furrows, be glad. Though earth is bare, One more seed is planted there', and its refrain, 'Love the Guest, Rose, Bird, Star, Lord is on the way.'

Another friend of my youth, Imogen Holst, had a dancing

'carol' step which would become a positive dance in itself when she was conducting. She possessed an inner joy which was infectious and funny and serious all at once. Both she and the editors of *The Oxford Book of Carols* were the last inheritors of Christian Socialism.

They were liberationists, who were able to trace back common freedoms and common worship through the years, and especially through the clutter of materialism, and via dancing songs.

Benton End

THE HISTORIAN or the naturalist views a place with maybe a knowledge that casts either a cloud or a brightness that even its residents lack. Thus myself shopping in Hadleigh, Suffolk (there is a Hadleigh, Essex), the day darkening because of its Counter-Reformation martyrs, who I see stumbling to the stake along Angel Street. Particularly the great Rowland Taylor, Rector of this wool-town and pupil of Erasmus, and who, they said, taught the weavers so well that he made it a little university.

As a boy, I would cycle to where he was burnt on the common, shocked and excited by his fate. Yet the Christmas shoppers mill along the pavements, and the corporation decorations move in the faint wind, and the lady in Boots has to decide whether I am a safe person to whom to sell razor blades.

Hadleigh High Street is a late-medieval dream of small palaces and big cottages on which the pargeting has been picked out with gold leaf. We – Vicky is with me – visit the Farm Shop for home-made bread and fine vegetables, after which I show her Benton End, the far happier scene of my youth, when I came to the East Anglian School of Painting and Drawing. It was a wonderful 'France in Suffolk' institution run by Sir Cedric Morris and his partner, Arthur Lett-Haines. Also a superb iris garden.

The ancient structure hung over the River Brett, and was full of students who were being unashamedly taught, either in the manner of the late Impressionists or in the style of the early 20th-century Modernists. The grounds sprouted easels and stretched way back. A bell clanged for tea. 'You're not an artist,' they said. 'You are a writer. Write our catalogues.' It was a kind of bliss.

The enemy was the bourgeoisie and his – in Suffolk, at the time, more likely her – values; for Cedric and Lett-Haines were very old and very witty about ancient struggles. Vicky and I sat in the car, looking at the silent garden, the tall windows shining in the patched walls as the sun went down, the beautiful, lumbering old dwelling settling once more for this night. And I imagined old whiffs of garlic and red wine, turpentine and paint, and old voices – somewhat grand – telling tales out of school.

Hadleigh was where Fr Hugh Rose convened the Tractarian movement. Confusingly, its Rectors are Deans of Bocking, and its church is an archiepiscopate peculiar. Do the holding-hands lovers in the High Street know this? On the way home, we visit a perfect village bookshop for a gossip and a celebration; for such delights are more likely to be closing down than recently opened. It, too, faces the westering sun.

Can I get more books into Bottengoms Farm? That is the question. Whole walls of them topple about. Possibly a few slender poets. The bookseller himself is a poet. I tell him how Boswell and Dr Johnson met in a London bookshop – the one so youthful, the other so ancient, if only in his 50s; for multiple failings were distressing that mighty frame. Johnson and Taylor had presence, majesty. The earth is the greater for their birth, their loud voices, their brave opinions, their teachings, their weightiness.

But what weather. It is keeping the leaves on the trees, and deceiving the roses. It does not seem to be interested in finance.

On Christmas Eve

ON CHRISTMAS EVE, Ian will arrive from the Barbican, and Joachim from Berlin. Joachim will light the dinner-table candles, break a white bread roll in a snowy napkin, and say the prayers for the evening of the sabbath. Later, he will drive me to the midnight mass at Little Horkesley.

Henry, our Vicar, will be assisted by James, the chaplain of Chelmsford Prison. I will administer the cup. Ancient hands, young hands, kneeling forms. Our Saviour, not Joachim's. He is prayerful every day. He designs gardens, including the garden of the Holocaust Memorial in Berlin. When I hear him reciting the Shabbat psalm, I think, 'How could they!'

I think of Joseph, Mary, and Jesus reciting it, careful not to keep the expensive candles burning too long, careful with the words. After the midnight mass, early on Christmas morning, we sit by the dwindling fire and have a whisky, three old friends who write books. It is our December rite from times long past. Habit, pattern, devoted repetition. Different sacraments.

The main difference in an old farm-turned-house is the absence of creatures. A cat excepted. Pigs, horses and cows, chickens and ducks, would have been slumbering only a few yards from where we are still awake. Chomping and rustling, making their presence known. We would have gone around with the lantern to see that they were safe, before we went upstairs. There would have been a nice smell of muck, and much breathing. Christmas animals, they would have been – we would have told them so.

There were knitted sheep and oxen in the church crib. In the Middle Ages, the crib was placed behind the high altar, and two priests dressed as midwives attended it. People were very practical then. And very agricultural. Fields and barns, stock-yards and pastures, meadows and woods, seemed to have run into naves and chancels without so much as a by your leave.

Thomas Hardy saw the hobnailed boots of labourers strike sparks from the gravestones in the aisle on Christmas morning. There was no holiday for them, not even on such a day. Feeding, watering, going round, yet revelling; for

> Herdsmen beheld these angels bright –
> To them appeared with great light,
> And said, 'God's son is born this night.'

> This king is come to save his kind,
> In the scripture as we find;
> Therefore this song have we in mind:

> Thank, dear Lord, for thy great grace,
> Grant us the bliss to see thy face,
> Where we may sing to thy solace.

This was written in 1456. What language! Sometimes, I fancy I hear it in the farmhouse, used to send the children to sleep or to keep spirituality awake. Hugger-mugger it was then against the cold, the natal music firing the rooms. And there was all that food, which wouldn't keep. And tipsy wine from the hedges. And human love and beauty. And devilish aches and pains, it being winter. And draughts you could cut with a knife. And this little boy.